Religions
of the
World

Religions of the World

EARL SCHIPPER

CONTEMPORARY DISCUSSION SERIES

BAKER BOOK HOUSE

Grand Rapids, Michigan 49506

Contents

Religions of the World

1

Studying Non-Christian Religions

Two Viewpoints

When studying religions, one encounters two popular but unhelpful and misleading opinions about non-Christian religions. Those who hold to the first viewpoint consider all non-Christian religions as totally bereft of truth and virtue, without any awareness of God or His demands, and thus completely immersed in the blackness of total depravity. Those who hold to the second position see all religions as divergent paths to the same goal. Some religions, they claim, may be more correct, pure, or useful, but all are equally valid paths to a Supreme Power, God. According to this view, cultural differences alone determine which path a religious seeker will follow. But if a person follows one path diligently and sincerely, he or she will find God. Some religious liberals who maintain this position think the best reason for studying world religions is to select the outstanding features of each religion and incorporate these into a global religion—a collection of humanity's finest attempts to live in harmony with God. This viewpoint is called *cultural relativism*, because all paths are relative. Each one, if followed diligently, gives purpose to life, prepares one for death, and provides peace with whatever power governs the universe. Before studying the major non-Christian religions, let's critically examine these two viewpoints.

The First Viewpoint

The idea that non–Christian religions are misguided attempts to satisfy humanity's deepest spiritual needs is correct. Unfortunately, it is not considered polite in our pluralistic time for Christians to claim that they are basically right and followers of other religions are basically wrong. But if Christians affirm, as they do and as they must, that Jesus is the Christ, that salvation is by grace through Him alone, and that God is a personal God who solicits the love and worship of sinful humanity, then they must reject anyone or any religious system that denies these assertions. Further, the Bible considers the unredeemed of other faiths rebellious and opposed to God. Although God has given them witness of Himself, says the apostle Paul, they have suppressed God's truth in unrighteousness, worshiping and serving the creature rather than the Creator (Rom. 1:18, 25). However consistent and insightful a non-Christian religion may be, we cannot obscure the fact that non-Christian religions represent apostasy, a distortion of the revelation of God. But to what extent do we reject them? And what is the nature of this rejection? Shall we reject every teaching, every insight, every religious custom and moral precept?

If we consider every non-Christian religion nothing more than pagan falsehood, we neglect the scope and power of God's revelation to humanity. Truly God has given witness of Himself to all people. Whenever people reflect on the mysteries and meanings of life, they encounter disclosures of God that He makes through general revelation, special revelation, and the common grace of His Spirit. Let us examine briefly the biblical truths about God's revelation to all people.

General revelation. According to Psalm 19:1, "The heavens declare the glory of God" for all to see. And in Romans 1, the apostle Paul writes that people are "without excuse" because ". . . God's invisible qualities—his eternal power and divine nature—have been clearly seen, being understood from what has been made" (v. 20).

In addition, general revelation includes the accumulated wisdom of the ages, which has been disclosed through great thinkers, philosophers, and scientists. Although "their foolish hearts were darkened" (Rom. 1:21), God's eloquent revelations to this world kept breaking through.

Common grace. God's Holy Spirit is at work in the world, restraining, teaching, and reprimanding non-Christian people. The term *common grace* refers to this work of the Holy Spirit, Who ". . . without renewing the heart, exercises such a moral influence on man through His general and special

11

revelation, that sin is restrained, order is maintained in social life, and civil righteousness is promoted."[1] The Holy Spirit has powerfully and mercifully guided the minds of non-Christians to insights which are valuable, observations about human nature which are perceptive, and moral truths that are worth knowing. Whatever is valid, useful, and acceptable in non-Christian religions we attribute to the common goodness of God through His Holy Spirit—not to the earnest strivings of humanity. In this sense, we understand the comment John Calvin makes about Titus 1:12: "All truth is from God; and consequently, if wicked men have said anything that is true and just, we ought not to reject it, for it has come from God."

Special revelation. God has further revealed Himself by special revelation. Customarily, Christians have believed that God gave His special revelation exclusively to Jews and Christians. But when we consider that special revelation includes oral as well as written disclosures, and that oral disclosures existed centuries before Moses committed them to writing, we cannot so easily believe the influences of special revelation are this limited. Clearly, God has been revealing His moral demands, His call to repentance, and His plan of redemption—at least to some degree—to non-Christians from the time of the Egyptian Pharaohs. Judaism accepts the inspired Old Testament; Islam cherishes much Christian Scripture as inspired; and other religions incorporate frag-

1. Louis Berkhof, *Systematic Theology* (Grand Rapids: Eerdmans, 1953), p. 436.

ments of special revelation. The similar moral precepts of non-Christian religions may result from the influences of God's oral and written revelation on humanity.

These observations explain why, as Christians, we cannot condemn all teachings, practices, and moral precepts of non-Christian religions as worthless. With our minds open to the insights and moral values held by people of other religions, let us evaluate them (as we ought to evaluate our own) according to God's written revelation of truth.

In summary, we may view non-Christian religions as human response to God's revelation, even though disobedient and misdirected as a whole perspective. After the fall of humanity into sin, God did not leave Himself without witness to His alienated creatures. He kept alive in human minds a "sense of divinity," and humanity, unable to fence God out, responded to Him by positing gods around whom they constructed their religions. In all religions, therefore, we observe reciprocal movement: God has revealed Himself forcefully, and humans have an incurable need to respond. In other words, a study of non-Christian religions is a study of the ways humanity has responded to God's unrelenting revelation. Some elements of human response are erratic, incorrect, and distorted; other elements evidence keen spiritual insight and penetrating wisdom. The religious strivings of all people are attempts to fill the God-shaped void in the human heart by responding to God's revelation.

This fact, however, does not give non-Christian

religions a modified ability to save souls. Non-Christian religions are just that: not Christian. We may appreciate them in the same way we may admire the poetry of Kahlil Gibran or the insights of ancient philosophers. But we do not look to non-Christian religions to find the way to God. That way is found only in Jesus Christ.

The Second Viewpoint

The second popular misunderstanding—that all religions are to a greater or lesser degree valid—raises a basic question: What is the relationship of Christianity to non-Christian religions? The cultural relativist claims that each religion has its own character, suited to the people who follow it because of cultural, ethnic factors. The religion cannot be judged true or false. All religions, including Christianity, represent parallel ways in which people search for God. Let's examine this position more carefully.

The cultural relativist, while claiming that all religions contain some good (although some contain more than others), refuses to distinguish between true and false religion. Stressing the need for sympathetic understanding, the relativist recognizes no absolutes, no biblical standard by which to judge and evaluate beliefs. Our task, according to the relativist, is to survey the religions of the world and choose the loftiest elements of each. In responding to this position, we must refer to several biblical teachings.

First, the Bible does not teach the mere *superiority* of Christianity among faiths, as if all religions were members of a family of faiths. The Bible does not claim to be merely a better way, an improved way, or a divinely favored way—it is *the* way. Clearly, the Bible rejects the relativist's position in the testimony of Christ: "I am the way and the truth and the life. No one comes to the Father except through me" (John 14:6).

Second, the Bible does not present the insights of a person stirred by the need to seek God. Rather, biblical history discloses a plan of salvation which originates with God, is carried out by God, and will be concluded by God. Christianity is radically different from all other faiths in this respect.

Examine, for instance, the person of Jesus Christ. The Bible does not present Him as one who discovered some keen insight, as Buddha did while sitting under the banyan tree. Neither did He arrive at some truth through meditation in a cave, as Muhammad did. In fact, He is not represented in the Bible as a man seeking God, but rather as God seeking to save sinful humanity. "Jesus Christ is no mere prophet; he is certainly no mere hero or genius; he is not a spark struck off the human block; he is no mere man reaching up to God. He is God identifying himself with man; he represents an incursion into this world from another world; he is God incarnate. In him God has come to men completely, fully, finally. There cannot be a revelation beyond this revelation."[2]

We must conclude then that Christianity is not

2. Henry Stob, *Theological Reflections* (Grand Rapids: Eerdmans, 1981), p. 119.

one path among many by which people reach God. Rather, it is the good news that God has graciously entered human history, executing a plan to redeem sinful people through the loving ministry and sacrifice of His Son, Jesus the Christ.

We must, then, affirm the absolute truth of the Christian faith; carefully evaluate non-Christian religions, recognizing they are neither biblical nor valid; and acknowledge elements of non-Christian religions that evidence insightful response to God's revelation. This view, which most adequately represents the direction this study has taken, is clearly affirmed by Stephen Davis, who concludes:

> Christians do indeed affirm that God has worked and revealed himself in various ways among the people of the world. According to St. Paul (see Rom. 1:18–32; 2:12–16) some truths about God were "written in our hearts" by God. Thus it is not surprising to find impressive wisdom and deep piety in the various religious traditions. Nor is it surprising to find virtual unanimity at many points in ethics. But Christians insist that the supreme revelation of God to us, the fullest possible revelation of God we can comprehend, the one sure path to God, is the person Jesus Christ.[3]

Why Study Non-Christian Religions?

In addition to the biblical rationale for studying non-Christian religions, there are several practical reasons for this study.

3. "Christianity and Exclusivism," *The Reformed Journal*, June 1981, p. 11.

In our changing world, it is helpful to be informed about other people's beliefs, values, and ways of worship. This understanding benefits us in several ways. First, if Christians seek to help others confront the challenges of poverty, overpopulation, illiteracy, and other social problems, an understanding of non-Christian beliefs is essential. How futile it would be, for example, to address the problem of overpopulation and poverty in India without an understanding of the Hindu belief in the reverence for all life. Second, Christians in today's society have increased contact with members of non-Christian faiths. If the Christian understands the beliefs and background of the non-Christian, witnessing will be more focused and effective. Also, Christians who understand non-Christian religions can appreciate the mission program of the church, pray more specifically, and empathize with experiences of Christian missionaries.

Further, by comparing Christianity with other religions, Christians can sharpen their understanding of that which is unique to their own faith. Contrasting distortions and comparing similarities compels Christians to define and restate clearly their beliefs. The following examples illustrate this benefit of our study.

Belief in a supreme being. Hinduism teaches the existence of one supreme, impersonal cosmic force, named Brahma. Although Brahma can be meditated on, he cannot really be worshiped. Islam teaches the existence of one God, but the human relationship to this God (Allah) is one of detached duty and total submission, lacking any notion of an intimate and loving relationship.

Although Jews, Muslims, and Christians agree on the oneness of God, Christianity alone teaches His triune personality and His loving disposition to seek the redemption of the whole world. Christianity's perception of God also has the highest possible moral content: He is a loving heavenly Father who seeks the welfare, trust, obedience, love, and worship of sinful people.

Divine incarnation. Most Hindus believe that two deities, Krishna and Rama, assumed human form. Another deity, Vishnu, is believed to have entered many incarnations, including animal existences. None of these Hindu incarnations was morally perfect—in fact, some behaved scandalously during their incarnations. Classic Islam abhors the idea of an incarnation because Allah would then be forced to share his glory. Yet the modern Shi'ite sect of Islam maintains that Ali was a divine incarnation and true successor of Muhammad.

Christianity, in contrast, teaches the unique incarnation of Jesus Christ, the Word of God, manifested in a historic person, Jesus of Nazareth, whose moral character perfectly represented the character and purpose of one invisible, holy God. His incarnate life, death, and resurrection fully satisfied all requirements, so that God could reconcile the world to Himself, with a lofty, personal result for each of us—". . . by means of the physical death of his Son, God has made you his friends, in order to bring you, holy and pure and innocent, into his presence" (Col. 1:22, RSV).

Future life. Hinduism and Buddhism teach the doctrine of reincarnation, based on the dreaded and unavoidable law of karma, which states that a person's soul is reincarnated after death to become some other earthly life form—a lower or higher form, depending on one's behavior during the life immediately preceding the present one. Islam teaches a future judgment through which rewards and punishments will be administered. Heaven and hell are described with vivid pictures of sensual delights for the submissive and agonizing torments for the unsubmissive. Islam lacks the concept of heaven in which fellowship with God exists.

Christianity, however, while teaching that there will be a future judgment for all people, describes the redeemed people entering the increasing joy of closer fellowship with God and the unbelieving and unrepentant experiencing the consequences of separation from God. In addition, eternal life for the Christian begins in this life, when the sinner is regenerated, justified, and adopted as a child of God who lives in intimate fellowship with God. And the unbelieving, disobedient people suffer the consequences of separation from God which they have already chosen. Christians affirm the vindication of the final purposes of God in the teaching of Paul: "Do not be deceived: God cannot be mocked. A man reaps what he sows" (Gal. 6:7).

These examples clearly reveal how a study of non-Christian religions can enhance and heighten the deepest meanings of Christian truth.

Additional Sources of Information

Alexander, David, and P. Alexander. *Eerdman's Handbook to the Bible*. Grand Rapids: Wm. B. Eerdmans, 1973.

Van't Veer, M.B. *My God Is Yahweh*. St. Catharines, Ont.: Paideia Press, 1980.

Vos, Johannes. *A Christian Introduction to Religions of the World*. Grand Rapids: Baker Book House, 1965.

2

Hinduism

The sacred word *Om*, written in the Sanskrit language of India, is a Hindu symbol. Hindus repeat this word many times during meditation.

Hinduism may be the religion most misunderstood by the Western world. Because it has no founder, no uniform set of beliefs, no religious headquarters, no direct divine revelation, no defined religious commandments, and no way of salvation that is universal to all believers, Hinduism seems obscure and poorly defined. But as the religion of most of India's population, it is a major system of belief that is gaining popularity in the West as well. Three-fourths of the world's Hindus live in India, mostly in rural villages and small cities. Nearly all other Hindus dwell in nearby Indonesia, Sri Lanka (formerly Ceylon), Nepal, East Africa, and the Pacific islands. With more than 450 million followers, Hinduism is surpassed in numbers only by Christianity and Islam. Explaining where they live is simple; defining what they believe presents complex problems.

Hinduism is difficult to define because of its

diversity. Many Hindus worship demons, spirits, and assorted gods, usually selecting one of 330 million for their personal devotion. Others engage in profound meditation and mindbending study of ancient scriptures. Still others, usually professional people, believe that the dedicated acceptance of their vocation—doing a good job—constitutes their religious faith. Hinduism excludes no "way of salvation," and no one way is preferred over another. No religion provides greater diversity of faith or practice than Hinduism.

Who would guess that the following people are all members of the same religious faith?

A wandering holy man who lives in mountain caves, meditating and refusing to recall his past life, or even to remember his former name and occupation.

A group of worshipers prostrating themselves before a clay image of a goddess, then parading the image through the village, and finally tumbling the image into a pond amid cheerful shouting.

A woman carefully creating geometric designs on the ground with delicate lines of flour to feed the ants.

A priest chanting from dawn till dusk to assure good crops, using a chant which has been preserved for thousands of years.

A full-time student dedicating himself to the study of engineering.

A young man collapsing after hours of delirious chanting before an image of his favorite god.

A holy man in a psychological, religious trance, with only his right foot touching the ground while his crouched body remains motionless for several hours.

An old man achieving the goal of his life—to bathe in the Ganges River.

All these people are Hindus, and wherever people practice Hinduism these religious activities—and many more—take place.

To an outside observer, Hinduism may appear to be an amorphous, shapeless faith, full of contradictions and mystery. One might find it not only difficult to understand, but also hard to respect. But to the Hindu, there is one truth, sought by all people, which can be reached by an assortment of equally valid paths. Each person must choose the way that suits one best. When people of other faiths present their ideas and their methods of salvation, the Hindu will not attack them, but will assimilate them into Hinduism. It is this capacity to absorb competing religious beliefs that has shaped the Hindu religion. Hinduism is actually the product of penetration and absorption of various religious ideas.

Christian missionaries report that Hindus absorb even Christian beliefs. Some Hindus respect Jesus Christ as one of many incarnations of the god Vishnu. Others accept the belief in salvation by faith, but assimilate this belief into their own religious idea of *bhakti yoga* (the way of love and faith). Some regard Christ as the Savior who has come to restore the world to purity, and others call Christianity "the most brilliantly lit bhakti path," while remaining members of the Hindu faith! Let's trace some of the major historical developments of Hinduism.

23

Historical Developments

Dravidian Period

The name *Hindu* is derived from *Indus*, the name of a valley and a river where the earliest Hindus lived. Not until the twentieth century did the ancient Indus culture become known. Archaeologists discovered that an ancient civilization existed in the Indus Valley about 2500 B.C. Under strong leaders, various tribes of herders and farmers, called Dravidians, developed simple technical skills and formed a strong alliance. Together they constructed brick buildings, some three stories tall, laid out streets in a rectangular block pattern, and lined them with simple two- or three-room brick houses. Although there is still much to learn about these ancient people, early evidence suggests that they held the religious beliefs that were popular at the time. It was common to believe that all forms of life were sacred, even lowly insects. This belief led to a vast system of polytheism that included gods in both animal and human form. Local communities maintained loyalty to a village god, while also giving allegiance to a chief god whom they worshiped with various chants of praise.

The reason for the Dravidians' decline after a thousand years is unclear. Geologists think that natural disasters such as floods decreased population, leaving the Dravidians weak and vulnerable to attack. That attack came sometime around 1500 B.C., when the fair-skinned Aryans invaded the Indus Valley and conquered the Dravidians.

Aryan Period

The highly animistic religion of the invading Aryans contained the following beliefs.

Animism claims that all sorts of objects, living and nonliving, have spirits or individual souls. Animism explained why a corpse and a living being looked the same, but were different; the soul was gone. Animism also explained the mystery of dreams. The reason one could dream of activities removed in space and time from a person's material body was simple: the soul left the body.

Polytheism evolved as a response to the basic questions which puzzle humanity—"Where did we come from?" "Why do tornadoes happen?" "What is humanity?" In an attempt to find answers, the Aryans developed poetic stories called myths. The many gods of the Aryans had elaborate histories, told with dramatic flair. Sexual episodes, tense rivalries, and personal struggles among the gods were mythical attempts to explain the struggles and mysteries of human life.

Aryan worship of the gods included animal sacrifices and emotional rituals in which worshipers performed frantic dances before the gods until they passed out from exhaustion. The Aryans honored and praised the gods by chanting hymns which became known as *Vedas*. The Aryans believed the chants possessed special formulas or sounds which gave chanters supernatural power.

Another Aryan ritual included drinking *soma*, a liquid squeezed from the leaves of an unknown plant. The user experienced hallucinations and mind-altering experiences like those produced by LSD or angel dust. The Aryans thought such experiences united the worshiper with the gods.

By conquering the darker-skinned Dravidians, the Aryans taught the superiority of light skin. According to the Vedas, a primeval man had become a sacrifice from whom the world was created:

From his head came Brahman, the basis of all existence.

From his arms came the warriors.

From his body came the merchants and skilled workers.

From his feet came the servant class, naturally the conquered Dravidians.

Slaves and criminals were not included and were described as "outcasts" or "untouchables." This marked the beginning of the Hindu caste system which still exists, although religious leaders and government policies discourage it today.

Priestly Period

Over a period of centuries, the Vedas increased both in number and complexity of thought. To interpret the holy writings, a class of priests, called *Brahmins*, arose. From approximately 800 B.C. to 300 B.C., two collections of religious literature emerged to provide guidance for religious rituals.

The *Brahmanas* include regulations for sacrifices to the gods and commentaries on the prayers of the Vedas. They teach the existence of the supreme god, Brahma. Brahma is the personification of the eternal, unchanging World Spirit, Brahman, believed to be the ultimate spiritual reality undergirding all existence. Through prescribed rituals and sacrifices, the Brahmanas teach a person how to achieve union with this Cosmic Spirit.

The *Upanishads*, a parallel collection of scriptures, agree on the existence of Brahman, but differ from the Brahmanas. These contain freewheeling philosophical commentaries on the ideas of the Vedas. The Upanishads recommend that, in order to achieve union with Brahman, each individual must be devoted to strict asceticism and meditation. Because the Upanishads are abstract, most Hindus prefer the concrete practices of sacrifice and chanted prayers.

The Brahmanas contain priestly directions, while the Upanishads present a more prophetic, teaching emphasis. This sequence is similar to that of the Old Testament—first the priests, then the prophets. Perhaps ancient travelers unknowingly helped shape the holy writings of Hinduism.

Incarnation Period

The *Mahabharata*, a story told in a hundred thousand verses, is a group of writings developed between 100 B.C. and A.D. 500. It teaches the values of loyalty, truthfulness, and bravery through the story of an allegorical conflict between good and evil. The *Ramayana*, another group of writings, recounts the exploits of a deposed prince, Rama, who conquers the forces of evil through courage, modesty, and selflessness. These epic poems are dearly loved by all Hindus and, unlike the Vedas, which are reserved for members of the higher castes, these scriptures bring the Upanishads to the level of the common people. These epic poems shaped Hinduism in a number of ways.

First, Hinduism became more god-centered, and two gods emerged. Vishnu and Shiva joined Brahma as prominent deities. The common people could relate to these personal expressions of a remote, abstract Cosmic Force. As a result, devotion to a personal god became popular and worship took form in prayers, offerings, incense, music, images, and temples.

Second, the love between God and humanity was introduced by the best-known section of the Mahabharata, the *Bhagavad Gita* (Song of the Adorable One). Because this epic poem is revered by all Hindus and expresses the most universal religious emotions, the Bhagavad Gita is sometimes called the "gospel of Hinduism." The hero of this poem, Arjuna, receives encouragement and moral advice from a fellow warrior named Krishna. As the story develops, Krishna reveals to Arjuna his true identity: an incarnation of the Cosmic Force or Supreme Being. Krishna is portrayed as a loving, compassionate incarnation of God, who says,

Take My last word, My utmost meaning have!
Precious thou art to me; right well-beloved!
Listen! I tell thee for thy comfort this.
Give Me thy heart! adore Me! serve Me! cling
In faith and love and reverence to Me!

So shalt thou come to Me! I promise true.
For thou art sweet to Me! . . . Fly to Me alone!
Make Me thy single refuge! I will free
Thy soul from all its sins! Be of good cheer![1]

For the first time, the Cosmic Spirit enters human life and provides direct, concrete advice on how to live. As Arjuna faces the horror of war, Krishna comforts him by explaining the relation of this life to the eternal life to come:

. . . . for the wise in heart
Mourn not for those that live, nor those that
   die.
Nor I, nor thou, nor any one of these,
Ever was not, nor ever will not be,
For ever and for ever afterwards.
All that doth live, lives always! To man's frame
As there come infancy and youth and age,
So come there raisings-up and laying down
Of other and of other life-abodes,
Which the wise know, and fear not. This that
   irks—
Thy sense-life, thrilling to the elements—
Bringing thee heat and cold, sorrows and joys,
'Tis brief and mutable! . . .
Birthless and deathless and changeless
   remaineth the spirit for ever;
Death hath not touched it at all, dead though
   the house of it seems! . . .
Be mindful of thy name, and tremble not!
Nought better can betide a martial soul
Than lawful war; happy the warrior

1. *Bhagavad Gita: The Song Celestial* (New York: Heritage, 1965), pp. 116, 117.

To whom comes joy of battle . . . opening for
  him
A gateway unto Heav'n. Therefore arise . . .
  brace
Thine arm for conflict, nerve thy heart to
  meet—
As things alike to thee—pleasure or pain,
Profit or ruin, victory or defeat:
So minded, gird thee to the fight, for so
Thou shalt not sin![2]

The idea of divine incarnation made it possible
to worship the abstract gods of the past in the
forms of animals and heroic men, which were
now understood to be incarnations of the god
Vishnu. Eventually, as many as ten specific major
incarnations of Vishnu developed. The epic poems
produced new legends and a revival of primitive
practices.

The new legends included fantastic stories of
the gods and their wives. The wives of the trium-
virate (Brahma, Shiva, and Vishnu), were deserv-
ing of worship and praise. As rapidly as the legends developed, new sects formed, each devoted
to one of the gods or goddesses.

The new popularity of the gods brought a
renewal of unattractive practices from the past.
Wouldn't the gods appreciate "holy death" as
proof of one's devotion? This logic led to the practice of committing suicide in the name of one's
god. Widows burned as they gladly threw themselves on their deceased husbands' funeral pyres.
Animal and sometimes human sacrifices suppos-

2. *Ibid.*, pp. 9, 10, 11, 12.

edly appeased the gods. Fortunately, these excesses ceased when enlightened leaders denounced these forms of worship. Still, the practice of self-immolation persisted in Hindu villages well into the twentieth century, when it became forbidden by law. When the British colonized India in about 1800, they discouraged other primitive practices, such as child marriages arranged by parents, inferior treatment of women, marital segregation between castes, and radical discrimination against the untouchables.

The religion of Hinduism resulted from these varied influences. No wonder it is called a "museum of religions" or a "fellowship of faiths"! Hindus are free to believe what they choose, to practice what they prefer. Still, some basic ideas and beliefs remain to shape the Hindu faith.

Hindu Beliefs

To illustrate the contrast between Hindu beliefs and Christian beliefs, indicate whether the following statements are true or false.

1. T F The world began when God created it and will end at some future date when God completes His redemptive plan.

2. T F Life's meaning is found in day-to-day experiences and human relations where God wants me to serve.

31

3. T F The individual has no eternal importance in my religious faith.

4. T F The promise of continued life after death gives me peace and hope.

5. T F God helps individuals realize self-worth; each person is important.

6. T F God wants each person to help in making the world a better place.

7. T F The highest goal of the religious person is to cease to exist, to lose personal identity and consciousness.

8. T F The universe is perpetually created and recreated, and will keep going through this cycle forever.

9. T F Salvation means to fulfill my life and it makes human existence a beautiful thing.

10. T F Salvation means to escape any awareness of my individual existence, to escape this imperfect world.

Based on Hindu beliefs, a Hindu young person would have labeled statements 3, 7, 8, and 10 as true, and the others false.

James S. Haskins observes that Hindus "believe that there is no real meaning to human life and that the individual is not important. Their greatest fear is that life may continue in an endless cycle of births and rebirths on earth. Their greatest hope is that they will find a way to escape this eternal earthly life and unite with a universal spirit that is above both meaninglessness and meaning."[3] What Hindu beliefs have produced such an outlook?

Hindu World View

The Eastern concept of time, the world, and history differs significantly from the Western concept. The Western concept assumes that the world was created by God at a certain time. Since then, with purpose and design, God has governed and directed the world toward its destined fulfillment. Throughout history, God has worked with a loving, redeeming purpose, and at some future date all things, institutions, and people will reach their culmination in final judgment and eternal reward. The original creation, spoiled by sin, will be restored and become the new heaven and new earth of Revelation 21. The apostle Paul saw this purpose unfolding: "The creation waits in eager expectation for the sons of God to be revealed. For the creation was subjected to frustration, not by its own choice, but by the will of the one who subjected it, in hope that the creation itself will be liberated from its bondage to decay and brought into the glorious freedom of the children of God. We know that the whole creation has been groaning as in the pains of childbirth right up to the present time" (Rom. 8:19–22).

The Eastern view, on the other hand, regards the present universe as unending, filled with

3. *Religions* (Philadelphia and New York: Lippincott, 1973), p. 15.

countless worlds. Everything that happens has happened before and will happen again. Human history is but an infinitesimal blinking of an eye in a universal, constantly changing, never-ending cycle of birth and rebirth.

The Western mind thinks of time as a cross-country race. There is a beginning and a steady, straight progression to a finish line. In contrast, Hindus conceive of time as countless eternal laps around a track on which each person is locked into a cycle of birth and rebirth called *samsara*. The universe itself is trapped in this cycle. The present universe will endure for more than four billion years; then, like other universes before it, it will be replaced by another. The Eastern concept is sometimes called the cyclical view of history, while the Western is called the teleological view (*teleos* means "purpose"). Figure 1 illustrates both concepts.

The Human Predicament

Because Hindus believe that all forms of existence, including this present world and everything in it, are momentary and impermanent, they refer to them as *maya*. What we think we experience with our five senses is maya, or illusion. The experiences which crowd our days with school, assignments, tests, and dates are maya. So are sadness, happiness, anger, and depression.

The only true, eternal reality is Brahman or World Soul. So the goal of every Hindu is to break free of this imperfect world and achieve blissful union with Brahman. Everything that is real is

Figure 1

Cyclical View

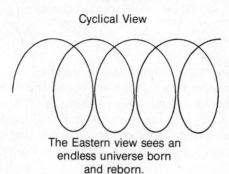

The Eastern view sees an
endless universe born
and reborn.

Teleological View

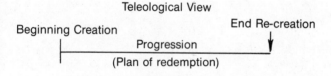

Beginning Creation   End Re-creation

Progression

(Plan of redemption)

The Western view sees a
beginning, a progression,
and an end.

Brahman. If something isn't Brahman, it doesn't exist. What we think we experience as reality is similar to what we think we experience in a dream; on waking we discover that our experience was an illusion.

Let's attempt to clarify the Hindu conception of the human predicament by use of a diagram (Figure 2). Start with a picture of an inverted ocean, labeling the ocean Brahman. Hindus call this World Soul, Cosmic Force, Impersonal Spirit, or the Only and Ultimate Reality.

35

Figure 2
Brahman—World Soul or Cosmic Force

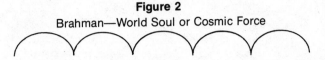

Now let's imagine that a drop of this ocean becomes separated from the ocean and resides as an individual soul within a living thing. Although technically this is not a soul, an individual *atman* is the essential core of life, a part of World Soul which is temporarily separated (see Figure 3).

Figure 3

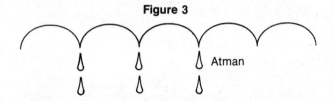

Once separated, the atman is trapped in the dreaded cycle of birth and rebirth into which all living things are locked. How can the individual atman achieve reunion with World Soul? Trapped in the cycle of samsara, the atman can be reborn into another form in the next life cycle. This process is called *reincarnation*. Technically, reincarnation means rebirth into a new existence at the same level as the previous one. The exact term for rebirth at a higher or lower level is *transmigration* ("to migrate across") of souls. Each atman in any life form seeks, through successive rebirths spanning countless cycles of time, to move upward to ultimate reunion with Brahman.

What determines the direction an atman will

take on reentry as a reincarnated life form? That depends on the karma which has been earned in the previous existence. The Law of Karma states: *From good must come good, from evil must come evil*. For each level of existence, there is a specific religious duty which must be followed for the accumulation of karma. The *dharma*, or religious duty, of a dog would be obedience—obeying its master and not biting innocent victims. For an elephant, dharma would involve nonviolence and service to higher forms of life. The human dharma is to live righteously in a social class or caste level. The atman is reborn into a higher or lower caste, depending on the amount of karma garnered by the performance of the defined religious duty. An animal may rise to human rebirth over a period of time—or all at once, if some heroic animal deed spared a human life. In contrast, a human can be reborn into a lower form of life such as a chicken, monkey, or dog. Because every atman will eventually find its way back to Brahman, there is no damnation or hell. However, the hold of samsara is so powerful, and the prolonged cycles of life are so meaningless and slow, that most Hindus are terrorized by samsara.

When high-caste Hindus escape from samsara, they experience release from limitations and difficulties of earthly existence. Any evidence of personal identity or selfhood is destroyed when the atman of living persons merge with World Soul. In this state, the holy one loses all sensation, no longer experiences emotions or needs, and loses the illusion of life. This union, called *nirvana*, is sometimes referred to as annihilation or "blowing out the candle of self." To achieve nirvana is the highest goal and the most difficult to attain. When Hindus believe that a holy man has achieved nirvana, his death is the cause for tremendous celebrations because he has been released from samsara. Such people, while alive, are called "silent ones" *(moksha)* for two reasons: they no longer exist in the same sense as ordinary mortals, having already extinguished their egos; and, the experience transcends human expression. Loss of individuality may seem undesirable to the Christian, but the devout Hindu seeks nirvana above and beyond any other experience or goal (see Figure 4).

The Paths of Salvation

To achieve union of the atman with Brahman, one can use a number of disciplines, paths, or methods of training. Each of the four yogas, or paths of salvation, is designed for a particular

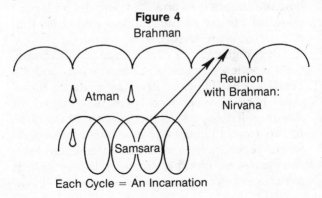

Figure 4
Brahman

Atman

Reunion with Brahman: Nirvana

Samsara

Each Cycle = An Incarnation

kind of person. Some are difficult, others are easy; but each Hindu selects one of these four yogas.

Karma Yoga (Way of Action or Good Work). With broad appeal to the masses, the way of action may take a little longer than others. But through good works, appropriate to one's caste, a person will gather karma to reenter life at a higher level in the next reincarnation.

In a general way, the following duties are required of one who selects this path:

temple worship, religious festivals, and prayers

respect and honor for the elderly

self-reliance

respect for all living things and refusal to kill any being for food or sport

injury of no one by word, thought, or deed

sexual abstinence (not commanded but encouraged as an incentive for extra karma)

Bhakti Yoga (Way of Love and Faith). Another of the easier paths calls for total devotion (love and faith) to one of the Hindu gods. A person not only may select which god will receive love and adoration, but also may select the most appealing way. Because the worship is often emotional and colorful, Bhakti Yoga is a favorite of the masses. They often portray the chosen god in gaudy costumes and lurid colors, and celebrations include everything from periods of prayer and fasting to days of sexual orgies and freewheeling festivities. Sincerity is important; the method of worship is not.

Because Hinduism has 330 million gods, there is a wide range of selection. Eighty percent of all Hindus are "village Hindus," meaning they honor some village god. But the three most popular gods are Brahma (Creator of the universe), Vishnu (Protector and Sustainer of life), and Shiva (the Destroyer). The two largest sects honor Vishnu and Shiva.

Shiva is usually portrayed with six arms, three eyes, and a blue throat, to represent his roles as destroyer, giver of wisdom, and giver of fertility. The third eye signifies wisdom or higher insights, and the blue throat results from swallowing the full cup of human sins. Worship of Shiva includes fertility rites in which evil spirits are warded off and exaggerated shapes of sex organs are exalted. Followers of Shiva wear horizontal bands of paint across their foreheads.

Vishnu appears kind, compassionate, and understanding. For this reason, Vishnu is believed to have come to earth in various incarnations or *avatars*. Hindus believe that Vishnu assumes a human or animal body and visits earth as a savior in times of world crisis. For example, a giant turtle that once saved humanity was Vishnu incarnate. Krishna (Lord of the group called Hare Krishna) was the eighth incarnation of Vishnu. Some Hindus have incorporated Christianity by making Christ the tenth avatar of Vishnu.

When Hindus are asked whether their worship of so many gods and goddesses by means of images constitutes idolatry, the more educated might suggest that images or idols, as well as the 330 million gods, are merely pointers or visual aids to the one Ultimate Reality, Brahman.

Jnana Yoga (Way of Knowledge). Designed for the most intelligent, the way of intellect or knowledge requires the teaching of *guru* (religious teachers) and includes prolonged periods of intense meditation and deep study of the Vedas and Upanishads. Stressing the philosophical ideas of these scriptures, the yogins who practice the way of knowledge tend to become intellectually sophisticated and to consider themselves better than the masses who follow easier paths.

Raja Yoga (Way of Meditation). The least popular path to salvation, and the most difficult, considers a person a four-layered being:

1. the physical exterior (maya)
2. the personality—personal consciousness
3. the subconscious—known only to those who make an effort to discover it
4. the atman—the core of personal being, the piece of World Soul

To make contact with atman, the person who practices the way of meditation must "peel away" the three upper layers to expose the core. The discipline required for this path to salvation is so demanding that certain preparations must precede its start. During preparation, the yogin must abstain from theft, lying, greed, violence, and sexual thoughts. He must develop personal cleanliness, self-control, contentment, and deep philosophical thought. Also, the yogin must use five postures till they become second nature to him, since he will be required to maintain a single position for hours without feeling discomfort. Suggested breathing controls call for inhaling for sixteen counts, holding it for sixty-four, and exhaling for thirty-two counts.

Hindu Lifestyle

The Stages of Life for Men

By dividing the lives of men into four stages, Hinduism seeks to enhance the possibility of accumulating karma, and to better the chances of a higher reincarnation. Certain duties and attitudes are appropriate for each stage.

The first stage is the life of a student. At some point between the ages of eight and twelve, the Hindu male is initiated or confirmed into the Hindu faith. Beginning at that point, and for the next twelve years, he is a student. With the help of a guru, the Hindu male must apply himself diligently to study and avoid laziness and flighty behavior. At his initiation, each Hindu male receives the sacred thread, a lifelong memento of his spiritual rebirth.

The second stage is that of the householder and parent. Beginning at marriage, this stage marks the time when dedication to wife and family are appropriate. Developing his job position, rearing a family, and establishing a home occupy the Hindu man in his twenties and thirties. Toward the end of this period especially, one should begin to see the inadequacy of pleasure and success as life goals and should begin to serve others in the community.

The third stage is retirement. The arrival of his first grandchild marks the beginning of the stage in which the wise man will contemplate the deeper meaning of life. By this time, he should realize that his past deeds, however kind and worthy of merit, are impermanent. He should spend increasing amounts of time meditating, studying the scriptures, and praying, in an effort to lose self-identity through oneness with Brahman.

The fourth stage is withdrawal. If a person can achieve union with Brahman while alive, physical death becomes a trivial footnote. Having become a "silent one" (moksha), such an individual loses his personal identity, lives without wants or needs, abandons all earthly ambitions, and appears uncaring and out of touch with reality. He prefers not to reveal his former name and occupation. The holy man often leaves his home to wander about or reside in a new location, in a humble cottage or a mountain cave.

The Role of Women

Although modern India has raised the status of Hindu women, females have traditionally held a lowly place. Initiation into the Hindu religion and the stages of life have applied only to males for thousands of years. The "village Hindus" still retain traditional beliefs and downgrade the role of women. Among the guidelines for women's behavior, traditional Hindu beliefs state that:

1. As a girl, she must submit to her father; as a young bride, she must submit to her husband; and as a widow, she must submit to her sons. A woman may never make her own decisions.
2. A good wife is always cheerful and efficient, never wishes separation from her husband, and never does anything that is disagreeable to him.
3. After her husband dies, a good woman will never remarry or even mention the name of another man.
4. A wife has no right to her husband's property; if she acquires property, it automatically belongs to her husband. At his death, his male heirs inherit all of his property.

The Caste System

Although early society in India was divided along racial lines, later developments created caste divisions based on occupation and birth. There are four castes or social levels:

1. Brahmins: the priests and religious teachers
2. Kshatriyas: the rulers and soldiers
3. Vaishyas: the merchants and farmers
4. Sudras: the peasants and servants

Each of these four major social levels has been subdivided, and a complex system of three thousand subcastes has resulted.

A tragic result of the caste system has been the development of an outcast class called the *Untouchables*. One becomes a member of the Untouchables if he breaks the rules of his caste, although a person can also be born into the class. Hindus reserved what they considered the lowest occupations for the Untouchables: cutting hair, cleaning latrines, hauling garbage, repairing shoes, butchering, and delivering babies. Laws protecting the human rights of the Untouchables were passed in the 1950s. Visitors to India report, however, that the concept of untouchability remains strong in the rural areas of southern India.

Until recent times, the caste system virtually dictated a person's way of life in India. For example, it determined one's diet, style of dress, neighborhood, time of prayer, mate in marriage, and many other basic considerations. The first three castes were referred to as the "twice-born," a reference to their physical birth and their later initiation into the Hindu faith with the presentation of the sacred thread. The lowly Sudras were denied this privilege, and could only hope for improved status in a later incarnation. Indeed, it was forbidden that they should study the Vedas, and any unfortunate who accidentally heard these most sacred Scriptures being recited would have his ears filled with molten lead!

Whatever a person's caste, it was possible for him to be polluted, usually through some improper type of exposure to someone of a lower caste or an Untouchable. A Brahmin, for example, was not to drink water that had been carried, touched or otherwise polluted by an Untouchable. He could be polluted by the shadow of an Untouchable falling across his own, or even by the presence of his own son at the same dining table, before the boy had received a sacred thread in the initiation rite. There were minimum distances, measured in paces, which a person of lower caste had to maintain between himself and a person of higher caste, to avoid polluting the latter. Often, Untouchables were required to beat wooden clappers to warn of their approach, and they were forbidden to use public roads, lest their shadows defile any of the "twice-born" passing by.[4]

Worship

Before engaging in worship of any kind, the devout Hindu man washes himself with water as a symbol of cleansing and purification. Once he is prepared, his worship might include:

honoring his chosen god with gifts of food and flowers

chanting the name of a favorite god or a sacred formula called a *mantra* (Such formulas are believed to possess extraordinary powers and are obtained from a guru.)

placing food offerings into fire that has been blessed by a priest

rising before daybreak to greet the rising sun

worshiping at home before shelf idols (Every Hindu home has a place of worship with a shelf for idols and an incense burner.)

worshiping at temple ceremonies where trained priests carry on complex ritual sacrifices using water, fire, and flowers

4. Allen Evans, Riley Moynes, and Larry Martinello, *What Man Believes* (Toronto: McGraw-Hill Ryerson, 1973), p. 406.

Once again, no one way is recommended or preferred. Each man selects the method and style of worship that appeals to him, for all are considered equally valid.

The Ganges and Benares

Among the religious spots a Hindu wishes to visit, none is more highly revered than the Ganges River. Hindus believe that the waters of the sacred Ganges contain spiritual power to cure disease and wash away personal sins. A gathering of Hindus at the Ganges occurs every twelve years at the junction of the Ganges and Jumna rivers. In 1954, the mass of pilgrims went out of control; as they rushed into the holy waters, five hundred Hindus were killed. Every Hindu wishes to wash in the Ganges as near to the time of death as possible. Hindus who visit the Ganges carry holy water home for use in personal and family worship.

Located on the Ganges River, the city of Benares is the place Hindus wish to visit at least once in their lifetime, and the place where they hope to die. Those who die here have advanced significantly toward union with Brahman, so their deaths don't call for mourning but festivity. The dead are cremated and their ashes are scattered on the water. The holiest of men, such as the moksha, are not cremated; their bodies are weighted down and slipped into the river to symbolize the way the atman returns to Brahman.

Sacred Animals

Because all forms of life have an essential core or atman, Hindus revere them all. Since ancient times, certain animals have received special honor:

cobras, because they are believed to enhance fertility

monkeys, because the epic poems tell how the monkey god helped Rama

elephants, because Vishnu once came to earth as an elephant, and because they are believed to bring rain and good fortune

cattle, which are revered above all animals and are free to roam the streets of India (Some Hindus decorate cows as an act of worship and honor. To understand such reverence for the cow, we should remember that the cow has been the main source of dairy foods and fuel in India for many, many centuries.)

As a result of the Hindu reverence for cattle, eating beef is ranked among the worst sins. A Brahmin who eats beef will remain in a stagnant state after death for as many years as the cow had hairs! Helping sick animals is praiseworthy. Wealthy men sometimes donate money to establish "nursing stables" for the care of old cows, an act which gains considerable karma.

Krishna in North America

At one time, the missionaries of Europe and America thought that Hindus would abandon faith in an impersonal principle (monism) for belief in one God (monotheism), who revealed Himself through Jesus Christ and provided the one God-given path of salvation. However, the opposite happened. Led by men like Mahatma Gandhi, the Hindu faith experienced a resurgence and has recently gained popularity in North America.

Especially popular among young people in Canada, the United States, and Europe, the Hare Krishna cult of Hinduism has steadily gained converts. Because Hinduism tolerates varied beliefs, represents a search for spiritual liberation, and disdains material and worldly things, the alienated youth of industrial nations find the Hare Krishna cult appealing. In the early 1970s, George Harrison went off the charts with his song "My Sweet Lord," dedicated to the Hindu god, Krishna. Not until the concluding bars did the lyrics reveal that the object of adoration was the god of the epic poem, the Bhagavad Gita.

The Hare Krishna movement was begun in North America by A. C. Bhaktivedanta Swami Prabhupada. The sect is devoted exclusively to the god Krishna who, it is believed, assumed a human form five thousand years ago in the forest of Vrindaban in India. The stories of Krishna, found in the Bhagavad Gita, tell of a time when Krishna danced with a hundred women at one time, each convinced that he was devoted to her alone; and of Krishna's appearance to a troubled warrior, Arjuna, in which the idea of God's love for humanity and humanity's love for God were introduced. The primary goal of a Hare Krishna adherent is total surrender to Krishna.

The beliefs of Hare Krishna originated with Swami Prabhupada, who came to New York City in 1965 and began chanting the names of Krishna, to the accompaniment of cymbals, on the streets of eastern New York. He began promoting a form of Hinduism formally known as the International Society for Krishna Consciousness. Within a year a temple was established in New York City, and within five years Hare Krishna chanters had spread to every major city in Canada and the United States. They distribute their magazine, *Back to Godhead*, at airports and street corners. Until his death in 1977, Swami Prabhupada was treated with the highest reverence, often referred to by his followers as "His Divine Grace."

Our basic problem, according to Hare Krishna, is impure consciousness, an ignorance and lack of concern for what we really are. We tend to think of ourselves as students, athletes, musicians, and so on, but we rarely seek the deepest answers to the question, "Who am I?" The deep truths, called absolute truth by Hare Krishna members, are found in the Bhagavad Gita, which is interpreted literally as a record of absolute divine truth.

Absolute truth reveals that every person is a servant of Krishna. All have had countless births in the past and will remain in the cycle of birth and rebirth until given release by Krishna. Total dedication to the god Krishna enables a person to enter Krishna's society, the spiritual kingdom that lies beyond the material universe, where one is no longer subjected to reincarnations.

Chanting is one of the most important and well-known rituals of Hare Krishna. The purpose of chanting is to focus one's attention on Krishna alone in order to develop greater love for him and to achieve salvation through devotion and union with him. What is chanted is called the mantra, a series of Sanskrit holy words which form a divine formula for attaining union with Krishna. This formula, *Hare Krishna, Hare Krishna, Krishna Krishna, Hare Hare, Hare Rama, Hare Rama, Rama Rama, Hare Hare,* is chanted in a series of sixteen rounds each day by the members of Hare Krishna; a round consists of singing the mantra once on each of 108 prayer beads. But this chant is not to be performed privately; it must be chanted in the streets where outsiders can hear and see the devotion of the members.

Conclusion

With its remarkable capacity for absorbing facets of various religions, Hinduism has assimilated a broad spectrum of religious beliefs. Hinduism's vitality is revealed in these words of Ramakrishna:

God has made different religions to suit different aspirants, times and countries. All doctrines are only so many paths; . . . Indeed, one can reach God if one follows any one of the paths with whole-hearted devotion. . . .

The Saviour is the messenger of God. . . . It is one and the same Saviour that, having plunged into the ocean of life, rises up in one place and is known as Krishna and diving down again rises in another place and is known as Christ. . . .

People partition off their lands by means of boundaries, but no one can partition off the all-embracing sky overhead. . . . So common man in ignorance says, "My religion is the only one, my religion is the best." But when his heart is illumined by true knowledge, he knows that above all these wars of sects and sectarians presides the one indivisible, eternal, all-knowing bliss. . . .[5]

Questions

1. Compare the biblical teaching of salvation by grace (Eph. 2:8–9) with the four yogas of Hinduism.
2. Discuss the effects of Hinduism on the social and economic conditions of India.
3. Hindus claim that a person can retain the Christian faith and still become a Hindu. Do you agree with this?
4. Hindus say that Jesus is not the only way to our eternal hope. What is your reply to this? See Acts 4:12, John 14:6, and I John 5:11–12.
5. A Peace Corps volunteer in India reports that Hindus rarely feel gratitude for the gift of life. Which Hindu beliefs might explain this?
6. India has an enormous problem with overpopulation and, as a result, hunger and starvation. What Hindu beliefs might contribute to the slow acceptance of birth-control measures?

5. Huston Smith, *The Religions of Man* (New York: Harper and Row, 1958), pp. 86, 87. The quotation also appears in *The Sayings of Sri Ramakrishna*, compiled by Swami Abhedanada in 1903 (New York: The Vedante Society).

7. Some people have noted that Hinduism is very tolerant of other religions, but shows social intolerance within the religion itself. What evidence can you cite for this observation?
8. Hindus like statements such as, "You can't experience God by use of a book any more than you can experience the city of Benares by use of a road map." What means do Hindus use to experience World Soul? Through what means, besides books, have you come to know God?
9. In what specific ways do you think a Hindu would differ from a Western Christian in a competitive-sports situation? What might affect a Hindu's attitudes?
10. Define these terms:

a.	bhakti yoga	i.	atman
b.	Vedas	j.	samsara
c.	animism	k.	dharma
d.	caste	l.	karma
e.	Upanishads	m.	nirvana
f.	Vishnu	n.	moksha
g.	Shiva	o.	Brahman
h.	maya		

Additional Sources of Information

Books

Hinduism

Rice, Edward. *The Five Great Religions*. New York: Four Winds, 1973.
An attractive and readable book describing Hinduism and other religions.

Seeger, Elizabeth. *Eastern Religions*. New York: Thomas Y. Crowell, 1973.
The author focuses clearly on the origins, traditions, and teachings of Hinduism and other Eastern religions. Interesting; written for the average high-school student.

Smith, Huston. *The Religions of Man*. New York: Harper and Row, 1965.
Presents sympathetically the basic tenets of Hinduism and other religions.

Hare Krishna Movement

Back to the Godhead—The Magazine of the Hare Krishna Movement.
Copies can be obtained from members of the movement. You may have received them.

Daner, Francine. *The American Children of Krsna: Case Studies in Cultural Anthropology*. New York: Holt, Rinehart and Winston, 1976.
A study of the history, organization, and membership of the Hare Krishna movement. Several case histories are given.

Films

"Hindu World." Coronet Instructional Film, 1963.
This historical and cultural survey of Hinduism shows the various mental and physical disciplines called yoga. It examines the caste system, reincarnation, and the deep influence of religion on the Hindu way of life. Color. Eleven minutes.

"330 Million Gods." Time-Life, 1978.
Ronald Eyre traces the Hindu religious experience in two contrasting locations: in the holy city of Benares and in a small rural community. Part of television's "Long Search" series, the film focuses on the Hindu

approach to God. Color. Fifty-two minutes. Also available in video.

Filmstrip

"The World's Great Religions: Hinduism," Time-Life, 1957.
Portrays Hindu gods and philosophy, the caste system, the meaning of death, and the place of animals. Excellent photography. Comes with lecture notes. Color.

3

Buddhism

The restful expression on the face of this popular statue of Buddha reflects the Buddhist ideal of detachment from desires and possessions.

Joe was born into an upper-middle-class family and grew up in an affluent suburb where many professional people lived. When he was seventeen, his parents helped him buy his own car, complete with the latest accessories. The high incomes of his father, an accountant, and his mother, a real-estate saleswoman, permitted the family to spend summers at a lakeside cottage. No necessity or luxury was denied them. The family owned a large four-bedroom home, three late-model cars, four television sets, two stereos, one high-power inboard speedboat, one twenty-foot Catalina sailboat, one motorcycle, and five bicycles.

Joe attended college in a city with a population of nearly two million. One of his professors had arranged for some students to take a "weekend plunge." Volunteer students were to be dropped off at a designated area called Five Points with a few dollars in their pockets and nothing more.

From six o'clock Friday evening until six o'clock Sunday evening, the students were expected to plunge into the Five Points culture. Joe signed up.

For forty-eight hours Joe wandered, grubbed, begged, and struggled through the jungle-life of the blighted slum. Five Points revealed a part of the world he had never known: destitute derelicts, sleazy prostitutes, ruthless street gangs, confused old people, and street-wise children. The debris, the noise, the theft, the pushers, the poverty—all broke through his comfortable upper-class values and forced him to recognize the violent, poverty-ridden side of life. When the plunge ended, Joe had only begun to sort out his reactions.

Joe soon wrote to his parents, revealing the struggle his weekend plunge had precipitated. "I can't get those kids out of my mind," he wrote, "running the streets at 2 A.M., their parents sitting in bars, four kids in a bed, three beds in a bedroom. Older people are trapped—they can't move; they can't even get enough food to eat. I actually saw an old man sort out garbage with his cane. I don't think I'll ever be the same until I get a handle on why people have to live that way."

The Search for Meaning

Six centuries before the time of Christ, a young prince in India became disillusioned by human suffering in a similar way. Although it has been enhanced by legends, the basic story has probably remained intact. Before we investigate the legends, let's look at the story of the Indian prince, Siddhartha Gautama.

Born around 565 B.C., Siddhartha was reared in the finest style as a Hindu prince. Hindu priest-teachers, Brahmin, taught him the complex teaching of the Vedas and Upanishads, but Siddhartha was not as submissive as the priests would have liked. Inquisitive and curious, he probed their faith with questions. The Brahmin priests regarded his questioning as insolent and inappropriate; students should listen and believe, not ask questions. Perhaps Siddhartha's dislike for his priest-teachers had lifelong results, for he never respected them, either as teachers or as religious leaders.

A wise man informed Siddhartha's father that his son was destined for greatness. He would become either a powerful emperor or a religious leader who would remove sin and ignorance from the earth. Because he wanted Siddhartha to become a monarch, the father isolated his son within the luxury of the palace and the surrounding gardens. He feared that Siddhartha might see the world as it was and wish to become involved in some humanitarian service.

When Prince Siddhartha married Princess Yosodhara, they were given three beautiful castles, many servants, and anything else they wished for. For ten years they lived together, insulated from the social and physical defects of society. Celebrations and parties, complete with the finest cuisine, filled the weeks and years. Siddhartha and Yosodhara continued unaware of the racism, disease, and suffering among ordinary mortals.

Eventually, a son was born to them, making their lives complete. It seemed as though Siddhartha's father had been successful.

The Four Sights

According to the story, Siddhartha and his bodyguard took many hunting trips, during which the prince saw four sights: a sick man covered with sores, an old man wrinkled and decrepit, a corpse about to be cremated, and a holy man begging for alms.[1] At the sight of the first three, Siddhartha was devastated. If life included such sorrow, what was the use of living? And how could he live in luxury, partying and indulging himself, while people suffered such terrifying tragedies? Doubts and questions nagged the prince constantly, until he became spiritually disturbed with the shallow, self-serving life of the palace.

The Blessed Night of the Great Renunciation

The last party of Siddhartha's life started in the usual way. There were many guests, plenty to eat and drink, and of course dancing girls. Soon the light celebration became a wild, unrestrained party, in which the twenty-nine-year-old Siddhartha was a participant. After the party, Siddhartha was sickened by the frivolity and disgusted with the cheapness of the scene. Recollection of the wandering holy man and stir-

1. These are the famous "Four Sights" of Buddhism.

rings of discontent within himself left him no choice. Resolved to find an answer to the deeper questions of suffering and the meaning of life, the young prince slipped unnoticed out of the palace, leaving behind his wife and infant son. At the outskirts of the city he shaved his head, traded clothes with a beggar, and left on his quest for truth, never to return. Buddhists still celebrate this event, which they call the Blessed Night of the Great Renunciation.

The Ascetic Path

For nearly seven years, Siddhartha Gautama sought the ultimate wisdom. Gurus directed him to the Vedas, so he studied these scriptures diligently. But they offered no satisfactory explanation for human suffering. Five monks advised Gautama to follow the ascetic path—to starve and torture his body in order to gain spiritual wisdom. Joining them in earnest, Gautama slept on brambles, ate one grain of rice or one bean each day, and neglected and tortured his body until his spine could be seen poking through his stomach and his ribs stuck out like camel hooves. Still he pursued his goal in the belief that the extreme practice of raja yoga would reveal deep spiritual insights, as he had been taught. Finally—probably as he slipped in and out of consciousness—Gautama realized that no deeper insight was coming and that continued asceticism would result in a frustrating, useless death. Leaving the five monks, he set out to follow a new path.

Two decisions had affected Gautama's choice.

After careful reflection, he first decided that ultimate spiritual truth could not be found in self-indulgence. Years of palace life, during which he had experienced every comfort and been denied nothing, left him empty and dissatisfied. After he left the palace, years of self-torture and self-denial had left him confused and near death. As a result, he rejected both the path of self-indulgence and the path of asceticism, settling on a middle path between overindulgence and austerity.

Gautama's second decision was to pursue the quest for truth strictly on his own. Approaching his thirty-fifth birthday, he finally became aware that others had advised him to study the Vedas, to meditate, to live an ascetic life; but none of these methods had enabled either Gautama or his advisers to find new truth. At that point, Gautama began his solitary search for the meaning of suffering, without assistance from people, scriptures, or rituals. These two decisions later formed basic doctrines of Buddhism.

The Sacred Night

Slowly Gautama regained his health, and as he did, his mind settled. He realized that the wisdom and truth he sought were not hidden in some mystery-box of the world beyond. He concluded that all the wisdom and truth a man needs is within his own mind. While seated under a banyan tree on his thirty-fifth birthday, he resolved to remain there until all the implications of his discovery fell into place. Beginning that afternoon, Gautama sensed a deepened penetration of life's mystery; a breakthrough was coming. Legends attempting to describe the spiritual struggle suggest the wrenching tension he experienced.

> At this time the heavens, the earth, and all the spaces between the encircling zones of rock, were lit up with a supernatural splendour; whilst flowers and every kind of precious perfume fell down in thick profusion ... and whilst the earth shook six times, the Devas sang together in the midst of space, a joyous song, and rained down upon the earth every kind of sweet flower ... the blind received their sight, the deaf heard, and the dumb spake. Those who were bound in hell were released. . . .[2]

By morning, Gautama's mind had "pierced the bubble" of the universe. That night, during which Prince Siddhartha Gautama became Buddha (Enlightened One), is called the Sacred Night. The banyan tree under which he sat is known as the Bo Tree (Tree of Wisdom). This site, near Gaya in northern India, became a sacred place to his followers and remains to this day a favorite spot of devout Buddhist pilgrims.

Captivated by his discovery, Buddha felt riveted in his spot under the banyan tree. For several weeks he remained transfixed as he worked out the details of his insights. Finally he set out for Benares, more than a hundred miles away. Approaching the city, he met the five ascetic

2. *The Romantic Legend of Sakya Buddha*, trans. Samuel Beal (London: Trubner, 1875), pp. 224, 225.

monks with whom he had wandered; they became his first converts. The Buddhist scriptures record the oral tradition of Buddha's first sermon, "Setting the Wheel of Truth in Motion." Selected excerpts communicate the essence of his discovery:

Then the spot where he was seated began to heave and quake, and at the same time five hundred lion-thrones appeared in the garden. The world-honoured one, . . . with his legs crossed, without fear, in perfect composure . . . addressed the five [monks]: "Ye . . . who have left your homes, there are two things ye should finally and for ever renounce—all worldly sources of pleasure and bodily gratification, and also excessive mortification . . . which neither tend to self-profit nor the profit of others . . .

Reject and forsake places and modes of excessive penance; Check and entirely control sensuous gratifications; If a man is able to follow these two lines of conduct . . . He will attain the true way of eternal life.

. . . be assured that I have given up each of these erroneous methods, and this is the middle path to which I have attained; thus am I enlightened, thus my eyes are able to see and my mind to know, and therefore I have gained a condition of rest . . . and am in possession of complete spiritual life . . . and have reached Nirvana and am perfected. If . . . ye wish to reach this condition, ye must also use this middle path which I have used, and your eyes shall be opened, and wisdom shall spring up within, and you shall enjoy rest and reach Nirvana, and

the eight paths of holiness.... Then it was ...
wisdom was born in me, I was able to see, my
mind no longer confused or fickle, I obtained deliverance.... I have now reached my last birth; here-
after there is no more individual existence for me."[3]

The Legends

Many legends have arisen since Gautama's
time, mainly because scriptures were not orga-
nized or written until six hundred years after his
death. Oral traditions, kept alive in monasteries
and passed down through generations, formed
legends and myths about Gautama. One must
understand, however, that these legends were not
attempts to retrieve historical, biographical
details about the person and life of Gautama, any
more than images of Buddha purport to be a
physical likeness. The literary images were created primarily to portray the commanding power
of his insights and to invoke trust in his teachings.
Understanding them in this context, let's examine
a few of the legends.

Birth legends. Maha Maya, Gautama's mother,
became pregnant in this way: She dreamed that
she was taken into the mountains and bathed in
a crystal pure lake. Then a sacred white elephant
appeared, carrying a white lotus flower. When the
white lotus flower touched the reclining Maha
Maya, she became pregnant, although she had
not had sexual relations for thirty-two months.

Several miraculous events accompanied Gau-

3. *Romantic Legend of Sakya Buddha*, pp. 251, 252, 253.

tama's conception. Rivers stopped flowing, the sick became well, the fires went out in hell, the weather everywhere became fair, and lotus flowers rained from the sky.

When Siddhartha was born, he immediately began talking, and he stood up and walked several steps in each direction—north, south, east, and west. In each footprint, lotus flowers sprouted and blossomed miraculously.

Tea ceremony. One day as the Buddha was meditating, he became drowsy, which irritated him. Unable to keep his eyes open, he cut off his eyelids and hurled them to the ground. Instantly tea plants sprouted up, presumably to provide leaves for a cup of tea which would awaken him for the discipline of meditation. The tea ceremony practiced by some Buddhists is derived from this legend.

Gospel parallels. Some legends which developed during the first century tell of events in Buddha's life which correspond roughly to events in the life of Christ. Many believe that the earliest Christians to reach India, the Thomas Christians, provided the basis for these stories. Although Buddha disregarded claims of supernatural power, we shall note how the followers of Buddha transcended both the claims and wishes of Siddhartha Gautama. Among these legends are the following:

Buddha fasted for a forty-nine-day period, during which he was tempted to turn the Himalayas into gold.

Buddha performed thirty-two healing miracles.

Buddha fed five hundred people with a small cake.

Twelve followers surrounded Buddha, one of whom walked on the water, and one of whom conspired to betray him.

On the day of Buddha's death, there was an earthquake.

The Death of Buddha

Buddha and his followers had spread the teachings of the enlightenment throughout India for nearly forty-five years when Buddha, at seventy-nine years of age, became ill. Buddha's constant advice to his disciples was, "Within yourself lies salvation," or, "You are the Buddha." On the verge of death, he gathered his followers for his last words, urging them to be their own lights, independent of any help outside of their own minds, and to work out their salvation with personal diligence.

Although Buddha had requested that his cremated remains not be revered or honored, the ashes were distributed among rulers and kingdoms where important events in the life of Buddha had occurred: at his birthplace, at Gaya where he became enlightened, and at Benares where he preached his first sermon. Years later, monuments and shrines called *stupas* were built to house the many relics of Buddha and his followers. Given his lifelong disdain for external helps, Buddha would doubtless object to the reverence Buddhists have for his remains.

Buddhist Doctrines

Hindu Beliefs

As a high-ranking member of the Kshatriya caste, second only to the Brahmin caste, Prince Gautama was well indoctrinated with Hinduism. So the logical way to begin a study of Buddhism is to explore the influence of Hinduism on Gautama.

Gautama rejected many Hindu beliefs. First, and perhaps most important, he rejected the Brahmin caste and all it stood for. He saw no value in external aids to spiritual discernment, so he rejected sacrifices, offerings to the gods, the use of temple rituals, the use of prayers, and the use of village gods in any form.

Second, Buddha repudiated the caste system, with its notion of human inequality based on status at birth. Instead, he emphasized individual responsibility.

Third, from Buddha's rejection of the caste system followed the belief that salvation could be achieved by more than a chosen few within the highest castes. Gautama rejected the concept that only a few could achieve salvation, considering it pessimistic, exclusive, and flatly contradictory to his experience. Enlightenment, he claimed, was available to all who looked within.

Fourth, Buddha rejected the Vedas and Upanishads as useful spiritual authorities, although the Upanishads did appeal to his thinking on certain issues.

Finally, Buddha rejected the metaphysical or

supernatural emphasis of Hinduism, because he was more interested in a way of living than in elaborate theologies.

There were, however, some Hindu beliefs that Gautama accepted, and these shaped the Buddhist faith.

Buddha retained the Hindu emphasis on the personal self pitted against material things, although he varied this emphasis slightly. While Hinduism stressed maya, the illusion of all material existence, Buddha preferred to emphasize the impermanence of all things.

Gautama also accepted the traditional beliefs of reincarnation and karma. Buddhism, however, emphasized rebirth and release from samsara, while abandoning the Hindu idea of the soul locked in endless cycles.

Finally, Buddhism endorses the practice of raja yoga, which prompted Gautama to believe in nirvana, although he did not recognize any godlike force beyond this present, impermanent existence.

Impermanence

Basic to Buddha's system of thought is the doctrine of impermanence. No such thing as being, essence, or soul exists. Because we crave permanence, we want to believe that we possess life, health, and homes when actually ownership is nothing but an illusion. Briefly stated, there is no being, only becoming.

This means, practically, that a person ultimately owns nothing; "Ownership" is a label for something that constantly changes. Life is a process of constant, perpetual change. Everything about life is impermanent, unstable, perishable, moving, aging, dying, breaking up.

This teaching, called the *no-soul doctrine*, maintains a human being is not a genuine personality, but only a transient gathering of desires and psychic tendencies. Just as the word *car* is a convenient name for a collection of wheels, frame, engine, carburetor, springs, and other parts, the word *person* is a convenient name for a temporary assembly of desires, thoughts, intellect, and emotions. Once the car is disassembled, it is no longer a car. And if the parts of a human personality are disassembled, that person is no longer a person. Every human being is only a temporary collection of parts which are in the process of being disassembled. Life then is not something we *possess*; it is a *process* in which we find ourselves. As we'll notice, this key idea undergirds other Buddhist doctrines.

Four Noble Truths

The core of Buddhist belief is contained in the Four Noble Truths, which expand Buddha's claim that he taught only two things: the existence of suffering and the way to escape suffering. Once we accept the impermanence of life, Buddhists claim, we will be able to understand these truths.

Life is suffering. Whatever you enjoy will pass away. Whatever human friendships you cherish will disappear. Whatever brings you happiness and contentment right now is in the process of dying, changing, dissipating. If you are a good athlete, you will become old and stiff. If you are pretty, you will become wrinkled. If you are bright, your intellectual powers will eventually blur. If you are eager to marry and raise a family, every child you bring into the world will die. If you have never been seriously ill, you surely will be. If you are pleased with your new car, it will be a cubic-meter chunk of steel within ten years. Life is suffering. All of human existence includes the element of suffering.

The cause of suffering is desire or craving. The fundamental human problem is caused by our craving for and attachment to things. We suffer because we crave. We crave pleasure, material possessions, fame, success, education, money, cars, action—all of which are impermanent. The poor crave wealth; the rich crave meaning. The athlete craves agility; the fan craves excitement. The student craves a grade; the teacher craves success. The ill crave health; the healthy crave a good time. The employee craves a raise; the employer craves profit. The Palestinians crave land; the Israelis crave security. Everyone is absorbed with personal cravings and desires for one thing or another.

To end suffering, one must eliminate desire. Thinking about our problems does not get rid of them. Once we understand their roots, and act on that understanding, we can eliminate suffering. This obviously means that elimination of suffering is directly related to our attitude and our approach to suffering. Let's attempt to understand this through three examples which provide both an illustration of suffering and a response based on the Four Noble Truths.

1. The United States and the countries of Europe have been faced with a critical shortage of energy due to the policies of the Organization of Petroleum Exporting Countries. Americans are disturbed about the cost of gasoline and the inability to travel as they have in the past.

What is the suffering in this example? People are angry and worried. Meanwhile, the government is straining to solve the problem. These are examples of suffering.

Why is this suffering occurring? Because people desire to go places and do things. Because public officials desire to be reelected. Because people desire to get what they think they deserve. Because families desire to go out for dinner. Because young people desire to take friends out to the away-from-home basketball game.

What desires need to be eliminated? The desire to be famous, successful, reelected. The desire to have fun, have excitement, and enjoy life. The desire to have, to get, to acquire, to satisfy wants.

What happens if we eliminate these desires? We accept what is, we submit to circumstances, we come to terms with ourselves. We will have peace! We won't complain about what is not. We will not be upset about those things which are impermanent anyhow!

2. Amy receives a phone call telling her that she didn't get the job that she applied for two weeks ago. This is the seventh company that has turned her down. She calls her husband at work to tell him the bad news. She begins to cry as she talks about how badly she wants to work. She is convinced she didn't get the job because she is overweight. She wishes she could lose weight. Her hus-

band tries to encourage her, but finds it hard to communicate his feelings. They say good-by and hang up. Amy turns on the television and begins to eat potato chips. Meanwhile, her husband finds it hard to concentrate on his work because he is concerned about Amy. They both have a miserable afternoon.

What is the suffering in this example? Amy suffers depression, loss of self-esteem, a feeling of uselessness. Her husband worries about her.

Why does this suffering occur? Because Amy desires a job, personal attractiveness, encouragement from her husband. Because Amy's husband wants Amy to feel encouraged, be happy, find work, and solve her weight problem.

What would happen if Amy and her husband would eliminate these desires? Amy's attitude would be: The way I look is impermanent, unimportant. Jobs are also impermanent. I will find other ways to occupy myself and be useful. Her husband's attitude? What I am is not determined by Amy's attitude. I will affirm myself, instead of letting Amy's passing moods and problems affect me and my work.

Problem solved. Both Amy and her husband would be able to find inner peace.

3. John had planned to buy the stereo he's been saving for, but it started to snow and his father felt that drifting snow made driving too hazardous. John was angry because he really wanted to buy his stereo. Because he couldn't get what he wanted, he sulked around the house, complaining, "What a mess! I hate winter!"

What is the suffering in this example? John must stay at home, cannot buy the stereo, is angry.

Why does John suffer? Because he desires his own way; he craves a new stereo.

And if John eliminates these desires? If his attitude changes and he accepts the weather and the opportunity to spend some time reading, the problem is solved. Imagine that John receives a phone call from Jane, who says, "Hey, John, it's snowing today. Let's go skiing." Suffering vanishes when craving ceases.

These simple examples show that people react to their environment and circumstance in two basic ways. One way is to insist that the environment change. Another way is to change one's attitude toward, and relationship with, the environment. The Buddhist approaches human suffering by believing that the nature of the world is conditioned by the mind. Through right understanding and attitude, one can construct a new relationship to the world. In the process of changing mental attitudes, one can change the environment as well.

To eliminate suffering, follow the Eightfold Path. In summary, Buddha taught that human beings are enslaved to their cravings for wealth, happiness, security, long life, fame, and a host of other desires. The realities of our existence, however, show that death is not the scissors which cuts life off in the end; it is part of every experience, part of the process of each life. By clinging to our desires for the impermanent, we condemn ourselves to samsara, the wheel of life, and to more and more miserable rebirths. Only by eliminating desires can we eliminate the suffering of frustration, poverty, illness, and death. We can obtain this ability only by following the Eightfold Path.

The Eightfold Path

1. *Right Knowledge*. This is basically the Four Noble Truths, and is more likely to be achieved if one associates with a trained holy man, to absorb his wisdom and his spirit of compassion and love.

2. *Right Aims*. Above all, one must resolve to make progress toward salvation.

3. *Right Speech*. Our speech reflects our character. We must especially avoid speaking false, obsence, slanderous and belittling words.

4. *Right Conduct*. Five precepts constitute the core of Buddhism's moral code: no killing, stealing, lying, committing of illicit sexual acts or consuming of intoxicants.

5. *Right Livelihood*. One's line of work should not make it impossible to observe the moral code. Some specific occupations which Buddha condemned included the slave dealer, butcher, prostitute and the trader in lethal weapons and substances.

6. *Right Effort*. One must have the will power to curb his desires and develop the required virtues.

7. *Right Mindfulness*. Buddha told his followers that what a person is stems from what he thinks. We must examine our behavior, and the thoughts from which it stems. By improving our thoughts, we should become more virtuous. Thus, our ignorance, the real cause of our sins, can be overcome.

8. *Right Meditation*. By this Buddha meant the practice of raja yoga in which, after proper mental and physical preparation, the truly devoted person breaks through to Nirvana.[4]

4. Allen Evans, Riley Moynes, and Larry Martinello, *What Man Believes* (Toronto: McGraw-Hill Ryerson, 1973), p. 147.

Buddha claimed that no rituals, gods, or any type of outside power can save human beings. The only obtainable salvation comes from understanding the Four Noble Truths and following the Eightfold Path.

The Supernatural

Some people hesitate to call Buddhism a religion at all, because its emphasis falls on true reflection, proper psychological attitude, and right ethical behavior, without reference to a divine being. Buddha rejected the authority of ancient scriptures and ordained religious leadership. Some aspects of this rejection were:

1. Rejection of prayer, of spiritism, and of emphasis on spiritual intervention in human life. It is claimed he once identified his followers as "those who do not work miracles."
2. Doubt in the existence of a human soul. Buddha taught that the human being is composed of five entities *(skandhas)*: body, feelings, ideas, consciousness, and collective thought. "Human being" is merely the name of that which results when these five are aggregated by the thread of life. When the thread is broken, the skandhas fall apart. They may come together again, and probably will, but no soul will be transferred to them. Only impressions made by karma will affect future rebirths.
3. Doubt in the importance of God. Speculation about matters of faith held little appeal for Gautama. It is reported that when asked about

creation or God, Gautama replied that time was better spent helping people with the realities of present life than engaging in idle speculation.

Contrary to Gautama's teaching, however, Buddhists have developed complicated forms of worship, and some have even deified Buddha himself. Ironically, the man who rejected idols has become the world's best-known idol, and the monks of Buddhism have often come to act as priests, the class of people Gautama considered useless.

Nirvana

For the Buddhist, there is a state beyond the bondage of birth and rebirth (samsara), a state of liberation or freedom called nirvana. The theory of karma (that every action and every intention has a consequence for good and evil) and the belief in samsara (that the shape of a lifetime depends on karma from the previous life) can be escaped or outgrown. In nirvana, the state of supreme bliss, there is neither self-consciousness nor personal identity; nirvana is the experience of "passionless peace." Achievement of nirvana releases one from the cycle of samsara, and puts a person beyond the reaches of karma. The word *nirvana* means literally "blowing out," and achieving nirvana consists of the extinction of the flames of desire and craving.

Buddhist Lifestyle

Monastic Practices

When a Buddhist boy is four, his parents surrender him to Buddhist monks, who initiate him into the monastic life. First, the monks dress him in the stylish clothes of Prince Gautama, then they strip him and give him the simple robe of the monk. They shave his head, and give him a begging bowl as a symbolic dramatization of the story of Gautama. Usually the young boy spends a night in the monastery. Later, at age nineteen or twenty, he will spend a period of several weeks in a monastery, during which he will consider becoming a full-fledged monk. A devout Buddhist family is extraordinarily proud when a son decides to become a monk.

When a young man decides to enter the monastery, he commits himself to lifelong poverty, celibacy, and "moral propriety." Those over twenty years of age pledge to observe 227 rules of discipline, while novices are expected to obey these ten:

1. Do not take life.
2. Do not steal.
3. Observe sexual chastity.
4. Do not lie.
5. Do not use alcohol or drugs.
6. Do not eat after noon.
7. Do not participate in entertainment.
8. Do not costume or perfume your body.
9. Do not sleep on a comfortable bed.
10. Do not accept money.

The ordained monk forfeits civic rights such as voting and running for public office, but he is also exempted from trials in courts of law for minor civil charges. The monk's only possessions are one undergarment, two yellow robes, a belt, a begging bowl, a small knife or razor, a needle, and a strainer (to strain his drinking water, lest he swallow and kill some minute creature).

The Buddhist monk who begs for food must observe strict rules in addition to fasting after noon: he must accept whatever is offered and never say thank you. According to the Buddhist, the giver should offer thanks for being given the opportunity to show generosity and accumulate karma.

The Role of Women

Although Buddha permitted women to become monks, Buddhists have never regarded females as equal to males. Owing perhaps to the Hindu culture that spawned Buddhism, women have an inferior role. Buddhist writings teach that women can obtain karma as well as men. However, they customarily must achieve rebirth as males before they can reach nirvana.

Arahat

The Buddhist's goal is to overcome desire by reorienting his life through disciplined meditation. If this goal is achieved, the Buddhist becomes an *arahat* or "worthy one." The Buddhist arahat is a saint who has overcome the attachments and enticements of worldly pursuits, has perceived the liberating freedom of nirvana, is tolerant and free from pride, and has risen beyond the power of karma and rebirth. The Buddhist would describe this victory over egoism by saying he has become a "not-self." Here is a description of an arahat:

> Long ago have I escaped from all the meshes of
>   the net;
> No more am I bound with the cords which bind
>   gods and men;
> My body has been released from all these
>   trammels,
> And I have conquered . . .
> The five pollutions that affect the human race—
> The power of beauty, sound, odour, taste, and
>   touch—
> These I have long since cast away and rejected,
> And in so doing I have conquered. . . .
> A man who has for ever destroyed the source
>   of evil desire,
> And left no longer in himself a seed of
>   covetousness,
> Who is calm and at rest, both in body and
>   soul—
> This man is . . .
> Cleansed thus from all personal defilement, and
>   coming out of the world,
> He is truly a homeless one—a disciple indeed.[5]

Sects of Buddhism

After Buddha died, his followers split into two very distinct sects. These sects are known as *Hin-*

5. *Romantic Legend of Sakya Buddha*, p. 286.

ayana (Little Raft) and *Mahayana* (Big Raft) Buddhism. The name *Little Raft* was given in derision to those who emphasized each person's effort to cross into nirvana without external aid of any kind. The other sect claimed to offer greater hope for the masses, and took the preferred name *Big Raft*. Hinayana Buddhism is found today primarily in Sri Lanka (Ceylon), Burma, Vietnam, Thailand, Kampuçhea, and Laos. Mahayana Buddhism has been adopted in Japan, Korea, China, Mongolia, and Tibet.

Hinayana (Little Raft)

Without a doubt, Hinayana reflects the original teachings of Buddha more faithfully than Mahayana. Preferring their own chosen name, Theravada (The Way of the Elders), over the name given to them, they retain the original teachings of Buddha. Key points are:

1. Individuals must save themselves.
2. The ideal way to attain nirvana is to enter the monastery and seek to become an arahat.
3. The highest virtue is wisdom *(bodhi)*. Once wisdom is attained, the arahat has reached the goal.
4. Buddha is not a god, but a great teacher—a guide in the search for truth within the self.
5. Sacrifice, prayers, temples, and speculation about gods and miracles are useless.

The Way of the Elders is an austere, intellectual faith which focuses on the individual's search for spiritual truth and offers little supportive companionship or emotional comfort.

Mahayana (Big Raft)

Feeling that Buddha's teaching appealed primarily to intellectual types, some followers expanded and developed a form of Buddhism which appealed to the common people. Many experts believe that other religions, Christianity particularly, shaped the beliefs of Mahayana Buddhism. For example, the influence of the Christian doctrine of the Trinity is obvious in the doctrine of the three bodies of Buddha. Compare these teachings:

1. Each person should help fellow humans find deliverance from ignorance and error.
2. One who has achieved the ideal religious life is a *bodhisattva* (one whose heart is wise). The bodhisattva can claim nirvana at will, but prefers to stay in the world to serve others.
3. The highest virtue is to attain *bodhi*, (wisdom), and then reject the salvation one has earned in order to show others the way.
4. Buddha has been given three bodies: a body of creation (Gautama), a body of delight (which he experienced as heavenly delight), and a body of law (part of Ultimate Being). Buddha and many bodhisattvas are divine beings to whom prayers, sacrifices, and honor should be given.

    Human salvation is not in one's own hands; one must rely on faith and the mercy of the gods.

5. Temples, sacrifices, festivals, images, and pilgrimages are helpful to oneself and to others.

Zen Buddhism

On one occasion, Buddha was reportedly asked to explain his beliefs. In response, he lifted a golden flower and gazed at it without saying a word. *Zen Buddhism* is derived from the belief that personal reflection on life is better than high-sounding discussions. The heart of Zen is the conviction that real truth can never be packaged in verbal forms; it can only be experienced through flashes of intuition called *satori*. Consequently, Zen followers disregard doctrine, scripture, prayer, and rituals, devoting themselves solely to a Zen brand of meditation. To cleanse one's mouth of the word *Buddha* is classic Zen advice.

Zen Buddhists believe that enlightenment comes in flashes of inspiration that follow prolonged meditation on mystic riddles or puzzles called *koans*. The beginner receives a koan from his teacher-monk who has already achieved satori. During a training program of at least ten years, the student must discipline his mind and body until he solves the koan. Periodically, the student seeks help from the teacher, perhaps to receive an additional koan, or to receive feedback. The teacher might help the student by yelling, slapping the student's face, or beating the student over the back with a heavy board.

There are hundreds of koans teachers can use to lead students to satori. Koans present impossible questions such as, "You know the sound of two hands clapping. Now what is the sound of one hand clapping?" or, "What is it that makes you answer when called?" Koans cannot, however, be solved through logic or intellect, and the Zen student eventually comes to an impasse—a mental logjam. At the precise moment when mental and emotional pressures combine with strength of will, there comes a flash of intuition, a long-awaited experience of floating outside one's body, of sighing, or of uproarious laughter. Central to the experience is the conclusion that the koan was irrational nonsense.

Questions

1. Suppose you could have written Siddhartha Gautama a letter soon after he saw the Four Sights. What would you, as a Christian, tell him about the meaning of suffering? Use Romans 8:18; I Corinthians 10:13; II Corinthians 1:5–7; and Hebrews 12:2, 6–13 to get started.
2. Some observers have noted that Buddhist ideas have hampered solutions to the problems of poverty and the population explosion. Is there any basis for this observation? What beliefs of Buddhism might delay solutions to such problems?
3. What specific Christian teachings might have influenced the beliefs of a Mahayana Buddhist?
4. The Buddhist concept of nirvana is described as "putting out the lamp of self" or "passionless peace." Contrast this with the biblical concept of heaven and the redeemed person. See John 14:1–3; Romans 8:22–24, 29–30; I Corinthians 15:35–57; Ephesians 2:6–9; Colossians 3:10.

5. Someone remarked, "Christians and Gautama have something in common—both reject the idea that miracles happen today." Do you agree? Why or why not?
6. Read Ecclesiastes 2. Do you think the writer felt as Gautama did about the impermanence of life? How is his conclusion (in Eccles. 12) different?

Additional Sources of Information

Books

Buddhism

Matsunami, Kodo. *Introducing Buddhism*. Rutland, VT: Charles E. Tuttle, 1976.
A lucid primer on the essential features of Buddhist thought, history, tradition, and action, this book is written by an "insider" who is convinced that his religion can contribute to the enrichment of world cultures.

Rice, Edward. *The Five Great Religions*. New York: Four Winds, 1973.
An attractive and readable book describing Buddhism and other religions.

Robinson, Richard H., and Johnson, Willard. *The Buddhist Religion: A Historical Introduction*. Second edition. Encino, CA: Dickenson, 1977.
An in-depth study of Buddhism—its founder, teachings, practices, and growth.

Seeger, Elizabeth. *Eastern Religions*. New York: Thomas Y. Crowell, 1973.
The author focuses clearly on the origins, traditions, and teachings of Buddhism and other Eastern religions. Interesting; written for the average high-school student.

Swearer, Donald K. *Buddhism*. Niles, IL: Argus Communications, 1977.
This beautifully illustrated paperback describes the beliefs and practices of Buddhism. The author has written several other books about Buddhism.

Zen Buddhism

Petersen, William J. *Those Curious New Cults*. Revised edition. New Canaan, CT: Keats, 1976.
Contains an interesting chapter about Zen.

Films

"Awareness." Rolf Forsberg. 1969. Available from Christian Schools International Film Services.
Explores the life and philosophy of Gautama. Shows the Japanese tea ceremony and other ways the Buddhist sense of awareness is practiced. Color. Twenty-two minutes.

"Buddhist World." Coronet Instructional Film, 1963.
A study of Buddhism through the life and teachings of Gautama.

"Footprints of Buddha." Time-Life, 1978.
Ronald Eyre takes the viewer to India and Sri Lanka to explore the type of Buddhism practiced in southeast Asia. He interviews various Buddhists, each offering from experience something to help the viewer understand Buddhism. Part of television's "Long Search" series. Color. Fifty-two minutes. Also available in video.

Filmstrip

"The World's Great Religions: Buddhism." Time-Life, 1957.
Portrays the life and teachings of Gautama and the major Buddhist groups today. Comes with lecture notes. Color.

4

Judaism

The six-pointed Star (or Shield) of David is an ancient Jewish symbol. It appears on the flag of Israel and is a dominant motif of the Jewish religion.

In an Old Testament story, the pagan Balaam was recruited by an enemy of Israel to curse the nation, thus insuring its defeat. However, when Balaam had prepared elaborate altars and sacrifices, he found himself unable to curse Israel. Instead he could only bless Israel, and he prophesied, ". . . lo, it is a people that dwelleth alone and is not reckoned among the nations" (Num. 23:9). His prophecy of the unique quality of the Jewish people has been fulfilled by the history of Israel.

Although Jews throughout the centuries have remained fixed to a common destiny, defining Judaism is difficult. Part of that difficulty is caused by the fact that a Jew converting to another faith is no longer considered a Jew, in spite of biological origins. Some Jewish leaders distinguish three types of Jews. A religious Jew is one who accepts the faith of Judaism. A cultural Jew is one who does not have religious affiliation but accepts the ethics, customs, and literature of

Judaism. A practical Jew is one who is regarded a Jew by the Jewish community. The Supreme Court of Israel refused to grant Israeli citizenship to a Roman Catholic monk who argued that both his parents were Jewish and that he had been reared as a Jew. The court held that when he enbraced Christianity, he ceased to be a Jew. In addition, the Jews have become widely dispersed. The *American Jewish Yearbook* reveals that more than half of the world's Jews live in North America.

The very existence of the nation of Israel is viewed by many people as a miracle of divine providence. During the years A.D. 70 to 1948, the Jews lived without a homeland, dispersed throughout the world. Their history is a saga of persecution, prejudice, and wandering. During the years 1933 to 1945, the number of Jews in the world was diminished by almost a third. Long ago Frederick II, King of Prussia, stated that the existence of the Jews was the only valid proof for the existence of God!

The contribution of the Jews to world culture and progress is without parallel. Less than one-half of one percent of the world's population is Jewish. Based on this statistic alone, one would expect a modest contribution to the great names in religion, science, literature, entertainment, economics, and philosophy. But more than ten percent of all Nobel prizes in physics, chemistry, and medicine have been awarded to Jews. More than one-fourth of the world's population venerates Karl Marx, a Jew whose writings form the basis for the political system of Communism. More than 800 million Christians honor the Jew, Jesus of Nazareth, as the Son of God, and credit another Jew, Saul of Tarsus, with organizing the Christian Church as God's unique apostle. Albert Einstein, another Jew, developed theoretical physics, which has brought about a revolution in space exploration and modern warfare. The Jewish psychoanalyst, Sigmund Freud, profoundly influenced the treatment of emotional and psychic disorders. Many of today's entertainers and comedians are Jews. Great nations which arose at the same time as Israel have totally disappeared. But the Jews, homeless for many centuries, have done more than survive; they have made contributions far out of proportion to their numbers.

Questions naturally arise as one thinks about the contributions of the Jews. How *did* they survive persecution by Christians, by Muslims, by Hitler? Why are their contributions so great while Judaism is one of the world's smallest religions, numbering about fourteen million adherents? What teachings or historical origins account for the uniqueness of Judaism? Perhaps a study of their beliefs will help you to form some answers to these questions.

Jewish Beliefs

Denominations

Judaism has three principal denominations: Orthodox, Conservative, and Reform.

Orthodox Jews are the most numerous, both in

North America and in Israel. They consider theirs the unaltered faith of the past three thousand years. They accept the Old Testament as the revealed will of God and insist that the dietary and Mosaic laws may not be compromised or adapted to cultures or times. Orthodox Jews observe the Sabbath strictly, maintain every detail of Old Testament dietary laws, have designated pews for each sex in the synagogue, and use only Hebrew in prayers and ceremonies.

Reform Jews, often called Liberal Jews, believe their faith must be adapted and accommodated to modern times. The only binding laws of the Bible are those which refer to one's moral improvement. While passionately concerned for social justice, Reform Jews do not practice strict dietary laws, ceremonies, or rituals which are "out of step" with the times. In contrast to Orthodox Jews, they do not observe the Sabbath strictly, largely ignore dietary laws, practice equality of the sexes in worship, and offer prayer in the language of the country in which they live. In some places the difference between Orthodox and Reform Jews is that the Orthodox Jews base their beliefs on faith while the Reform Jews base their beliefs on reason.

Conservative Jews resent being described as "in-between" Jews, but in fact they are more strict than the Reform Jews and less strict than the Orthodox. Following the pattern of Orthodox Judaism for the most part, Conservative Jews believe their religious traditions and laws must gradually evolve to meet the needs of Jews within varied cultures. To Conservative Jews, the Orthodox are extremely strict and old-fashioned, and the Reform Jews are radical and modern. The Conservative Jew observes dietary laws as much as possible, keeps the Sabbath laws "in the spirit" rather than "in the letter," and uses the vernacular in prayers and ceremonies of the synagogue.

While observing that more than half of the Jews are so thoroughly secularized that they regard the Old Testament laws as relics of the past and attend the synagogue mainly because it might do the children some good to know their roots, Louis Cassells also states, "Anyone who thinks that Orthodox Judaism is a fossil faith, taken seriously by a few grey-bearded rabbis, should read Herman Wouk's book *This Is My God*, a moving testimonial of what it means to be an Orthodox Jew in twentiety-century America."[1]

An anecdote illustrates the differences between the various groups within Judaism:

A group of Jewish farmers was concerned about the harvest of crops on the kibbutz in Israel. It seemed that the Sabbath was the only time that was exactly right for the harvest of a certain crop. But sharp differences arose because the Old Testament laws forbade harvesting of crops on the Sabbath, except in an enclosed area such as a greenhouse. When the time came for a decision, the Orthodox Jew suggested the farmers construct a framelike greenhouse apparatus attached to a tractor, so they could "harvest the crop within an enclosure" according to the laws of God. The Con-

1. *What's the Difference: A Comparison of Faiths Men Live By* (Garden City, NY: Doubleday, 1963), p. 37.

servative Jew reasoned, "If God sent good weather on the Sabbath, He must intend for the farmers to harvest on that day." And the Reform Jew offered his solution, "If the Sabbath has such nice weather, why not accept this as God's instructions to take the family on a Sabbath-picnic?"

Because Orthodox Jews are the most numerous and provide us with the clearest example of historic Judaism, we will confine our study mainly to the beliefs of Orthodox Judaism.

Nature of God

Many of the beliefs and practices of the Jews have been modified over the centuries, but the belief in the existence of one God has never been subject to doubt or question. A Jew may praise God, love God, be angry with God, quarrel with God, but may never be indifferent to God. The cornerstone of Judaism is the *Shemah*—the words of Moses, "Hear, O Israel: The LORD our God is one LORD" (Deut. 6:4).

As early as the time of the New Testament, a Jewish philosopher, Philo of Alexandria, summarized the entire faith of Judaism in five statements:

1. The belief in God
2. The belief that there is only one God
3. The belief that God created the world; but the world is not eternal
4. The belief that there is only one universe
5. The belief that God cares for the world and all its creatures

In the thirteenth century, a famous Jewish doctor and philosopher known as Maimonides condensed the basic beliefs of all Jews into thirteen articles of faith, which are parallel to the Christian Apostles' Creed. These are:

1. I believe with perfect faith that the Creator, blessed be His Name, is the Creator and Guide of everything that has been created, and He alone has made, does make, and will make all things.
2. I believe with perfect faith that the Creator, blessed be His Name, is One, and that there is no unity in any manner like unto His, and that He alone is our God, who was, and is, and will be.
3. I believe with perfect faith that the Creator, blessed be His Name, is not a body, and that He is free from all the properties of matter, and that He has not any form whatever.
4. I believe with perfect faith that the Creator, blessed be His Name, is the first and the last.
5. I believe with perfect faith that to the Creator, blessed be His Name, and to Him alone, it is right to pray, and that it is not right to pray to any being besides Him.
6. I believe with perfect faith that all the words of the prophets are true.
7. I believe with perfect faith that the prophecy of Moses, our teacher, peace be unto him, was true, and that he was the chief of the prophets, both of those who preceded and of those who followed him.
8. I believe with perfect faith that the whole

Torah, now in our possession, is the same that was given to Moses, our teacher, peace be unto him.

9. I believe with perfect faith that this Torah will not be changed, and that there will never by any other Law from the Creator, blessed be His Name.

10. I believe with perfect faith that the Creator, blessed be His Name, knows every deed of the children of men, and all their thoughts, as it is said. It is He that fashioned the hearts of them all, that gives need to all their works.

11. I believe with perfect faith that the Creator, blessed be His Name, rewards those that keep His commandments and punishes those that transgress them.

12. I believe with perfect faith in the coming of the Messiah; and, though he tarry, I will wait daily for his coming.

13. I believe with perfect faith that there will be a revival of the dead at the time when it shall please the Creator, blessed be His Name, and exalted be His Fame for ever and ever.

For Thy salvation I hope, O Lord.

Obviously, God is the focus of everything in the Jewish faith. Everything, to the Jew, centers on God: He created the world, He cares for it, He is one, and He shares His holiness with no other. He is also a moral God who should be approached with gratitude, humility, and reverence. He demands good from humanity and will punish those who are evil.

In contrast to Christianity, which emphasizes

God's love, Judaism emphasizes the justice of God. The three basic principles of the Jewish faith, contained in the revered Prayer Book, illustrate this.

Worship of God. From infancy, all Jewish children learn that God is one, that He is not to be represented by idols, and that He must be worshiped out of love, not out of fear.

Importance of learning. On the first day of school, traditional Jews are fed honey cakes shaped in the letters of the alphabet so they will associate learning with sweetness. The Jews have always maintained compulsory education, even for the poor and orphaned. Formal learning always begins with the words of the Shemah.

Required deeds. There is no Hebrew word for "charity," because we are *required* to care for the poor. Just as God is a God of justice, not a God of love, we must insist on justice for all people, Jew and Gentile alike.

God's Chosen People

Although many Jewish theologians are uncomfortable with it, the belief that the Jews are God's chosen people persists in traditional Judaism. Based on the promise of God to Abraham, ". . . and in thee shall all families of the earth be blessed . . ." (Gen. 12:3), Jews continue to believe that they were chosen to be a symbol to all people. Many non-Jews are offended by the Jews' claim to be a "chosen people," and some have used this claim as an excuse for anti-Semitism, calling this claim an example of spiritual arrogance and pride which has no place in a religious scheme that prizes humility.

But the Jews maintain that the Bible strongly testifies that God did choose the Jews, entering a covenant with them and setting them apart as His special people. Non-Jews fail to understand that being chosen has put an awesome burden on the Jewish people. Jews consider people who convert to Judaism particularly precious because they voluntarily take on themselves the burden of this responsibility.

What it meant to be God's chosen people was best understood by Israel's prophets, especially Amos who relayed this message from God to Israel: "You only have I known of all the families of the earth: therefore I will punish you for all your iniquities" (Amos 3:2). To be chosen implies a definite responsibility to become the instruments of God's will, to show humanity what God desires, and to be examples that all people can follow.

In summary, the belief persists that the Jews have more responsibilities and heavier burdens than others. If they fail to obey God, they have failed humanity. And if they carry out their duty to God and humanity, they have indeed been a blessing to all the families of the earth.

Messiah

The chief difference between Jews and Christians focuses on the meaning of the Old Testament Messiah. Traditional Jews believe that a great hero, anointed by leaders from the House of David, will lead the world out of chaos, war, and disorder into a period of peace, tranquillity, and lawfulness. They claim that God will send a Redeemer who will prevent the world from rushing headlong into destruction. He will not be a supernatural person or a God-man, but an extremely capable person who will bring about the restoration of the Jewish people and, as a result, the salvation of all people.

The conflict between Judaism and Christianity has centered around this concept of the Messiah for two reasons. First, Christians believe Jesus was the Messiah while the Jews regard Him as a pretender, a false Messiah. Second, Christians believe that salvation has been accomplished in Jesus Christ, while Jews wait for a salvation which will be revealed at the coming of the Messiah.

Human Dignity

According to Judaism, humans made in God's image *must* resemble God, who is both merciful and free to do what He wills. Being made in the image of God means, according to Judaism, that people have dignity: they are good; they are never hopelessly lost; and they are capable of choosing to become more just, kind, honest, and good. Because each human being has the dignity of the image of God and the responsibility to choose those things which are good, Jews do not believe they must convert non-Jews to their faith.

Suffering

After centuries of suffering, the Jews have affirmed its value, although at times their suffering appeared senseless and its value hidden. The famous Old Testament book of suffering, the Book of Job, was so highly regarded that the ancient Jews claimed Moses wrote it. In this dramatic poem, Job says,

> I cry unto thee, and thou dost not hear me;
>   I stand up, and thou regardest me not.
> Thou art become cruel to me:
>   with thy strong hand thou persecutest me.
> Thou liftest me up to the wind;
>   thou causest me to ride upon it, and
>   dissolvest my strength.
> For I know that thou wilt bring me to death,
>   and to the house appointed for all living.
> Surely no prayer availeth when he stretcheth
>   his hand,
>   though they cry in his destruction.
> Did not I weep for him that was in trouble?
>   was not my soul grieved for the poor?
> When I looked for good, then evil came unto
>   me:
>   and when I waited for light, there came
>   darkness. [Job 30:20–26]

After the Lord answers Job out of the whirlwind, Job's suffering is put in the context of God's greatness, as God asks:

> Where wast thou when I laid the foundations of
>   the earth?
> Hast thou commanded the morning since thy
>   days?
> Where is the way where light dwelleth?
> Canst thou bind the fetters of the Pleiades, or
>   loose the bands of Orion?

Knowest thou the ordinances of heaven? [Job
   38:4, 12, 19, 31, 33]

Doth the hawk fly by thy wisdom? [Job 39:26]

Canst thou draw out the leviathan with a hook?
   [Job 40:25]

Humbled and awed by the presence of God,
Job resolves the puzzle of suffering with this
prayer:

I know that thou canst do every thing, and that no
thought can be withheld from thee. Who is he that
hideth counsel without knowledge? Truly I have
uttered what I understood not; things too won-
derful for me, which I knew not. Hear, I beseech
thee, and I will speak: I will demand of thee, and
declare thou unto me. I have heard of thee by the
hearing of the ear: but now mine eye seeth thee.
Wherefore I abhor myself, and repent in dust and
ashes. [Job 42:2–6]

Although no one can explain the horrendous
suffering of the Jews throughout the centuries,
the stubborn belief that God is present has persisted. This awareness of God's presence in the
midst of suffering is illustrated in the concluding
paragraphs of André Schwartz-Bart's novel, *The
Last of the Just*, where he describes a scene in a
Nazi death camp:

When the layers of gas had covered everything,
there was silence in the dark room for perhaps a
minute, broken only by shrill, racking coughs and
the gasps of those too far gone in their agonies to

99

offer a devotion. And first a stream, then a cascade, an irrepressible, majestic torrent, the poem that through the smoke of fires and above the funeral pyres of history the Jews—who for two thousand years did not bear arms and who never had either missionary empires nor colored slaves—the old love poem that they traced in letters of blood on the earth's hard crust unfurled in the gas chamber, enveloped it, vanquished its somber, abysmal snickering: "SHEMA YISRAEL ADONOI ELOHENU ADONOI ECHOD . . . Hear, O Israel, the Lord is our God, the Lord is One. O Lord, by your grace you nourish the living, and by your great pity you resurrect the dead, and you uphold the weak, cure the sick, break the chains of slaves. And faithfully you keep your promises to those who sleep in the dust. Who is like unto you, O merciful Father, and who could be like unto you . . . ?"

The voices died one by one in the course of the unfinished poem. The dying children had already dug their nails into Ernie's thighs and Golda's embrace was already weaker, her kisses were blurred when, clinging fiercely to her beloved's neck, she exhaled a harsh sigh: "Then I'll never see you again? Never again?"

Ernie managed to spit up the needle of fire jabbing at his throat, and as the woman's body slumped against him, its eyes wide in the opaque night, he shouted against the unconscious Golda's ear, "In a little while, *I swear it!*" And then he knew that he could do nothing more for anyone in the world, and in the flash that preceded his own annihilation he remembered, happily, the legend of Rabbi Chanina ben Teradion, as Mordecai had joyfully recited it: "When the gentle rabbi, wrapped in the scrolls of the Torah, was flung upon the pyre by the Romans for having taught the Law, and when they lit the fagots, the branches still green to make his torture last, his pupils said, 'Master, what do you see?' And Rabbi Chanina answered, 'I see the parchment burning, but the letters are taking wing.' "—"*Ah, yes, surely, the letters are taking wing,*" Ernie repeated as the flame blazing in his chest rose suddenly to his head. With dying arms he embraced Golda's body in an already unconscious gesture of loving protection, and they were found that way half an hour later by the team of *Sonderkommando* responsible for burning the Jews in the crematory ovens. And so it was for millions, who turned from *Luftmenschen* into *Luft*. I shall not translate. So this story will not finish with some to be visited in memoriam. For the smoke that rises from crematoriums obeys physical laws like any other: the particles come together and disperse according to the wind that propels them. The only pilgrimage, estimable reader, would be to look with sadness at a stormy sky now and then.

And praised. *Auschwitz*. Be. *Maidanek*. The Lord. *Treblinka*. And praised. *Buchenwald*. Be. *Mauthausen*. The Lord. *Belzec*. And praised. *Sobibor*. Be. *Chelmno*. The Lord. *Ponary*. And praised. *Theresientadt*. Be. *Warsaw*. The Lord. *Vilna*. And praised. *Skarzysko*. Be. *Bergen-Belsen*. The Lord. *Janow*. And praised. *Dora*. Be. *Neuengamme*. The Lord. *Pustkow*. And praised . . .

Yes, at times one's heart could break in sorrow. But often too, preferably in the evening, I can't help thinking that Ernie Levy, dead six million times, is still alive somewhere, I don't know where.

... yesterday, as I stood in the street trembling in despair, rooted to the spot, a drop of pity fell from above upon my face. But there was no breeze in the air, no cloud in the sky. ... There was only a presence.[2]

Sources of Belief

Judaism has always been a religion of "The Book," meaning the Old Testament, which is divided into three parts: the Law or Torah, the first five books of Moses; the Prophets, including books of history; and the Writings. Of these three, the most important by far is the Torah, which is called the "true foundation of the Jewish faith." In the Torah, God spoke His pure message in form and detail which has never been superseded or revoked. The second source of belief is a set of writings which have been handed down, added to, and explained throughout Jewish history. These are called the *Talmud* or wisdom literature.

The Torah

The word *Torah* is used in two ways. Broadly, it has come to refer to a way of life and is synonymous with learning and wisdom. In a narrower sense, the Torah consists of the five books of Moses, also called the Pentateuch. Kept in the Ark of every synagogue, a portion of the Torah is read aloud every Sabbath during worship. Every

2. (New York: Atheneum, 1960), pp. 373–374.

worshiper rises when the Torah is taken from the Ark, and pious Jews cherish the supreme act of worship—kissing the Torah by touching their prayer shawl to the scroll, then to their lips. The Torah is the most sacred object in Jewish worship. By following the moral and dietary laws of the Torah, a person will be guided to righteousness in this life and to heaven in the life to come. To the Jew, the Torah is Life.

The Talmud

The Talmud consists of sixty-three books which interpret and explain the Torah. All the precious truths and traditions were gathered together in these volumes, completed about A.D. 500. Many parables, anecdotes, epigrams, historical notes, and applications of the Torah make the Talmud invaluable to the Jew. Since the fifth century, wise rabbis have contributed time-honored sayings and folklore which have provided practical application of Jewish truths for daily living. Many Jews live under the "Table Prepared," which was compiled in the sixteenth century. Together, all these sayings of inspired teachers are called the wisdom literature.

Jewish Lifestyle

Folklore

Some fascinating insights into Jewish values and deeply-ingrained folkways are illustrated in these examples.

On drunkenness. To warn against the evils of drinking, a story is told that Satan brought a lamb, a lion, a pig, and an ape to the vineyard which Noah had planted. This was to be a sign that before a man drinks wine, he is as weak as a sheep. If he drinks just enough, he becomes as strong as a lion. If he drinks too much, he becomes like a pig wallowing in the mud, and if he becomes drunk, he hangs like an ape and speaks folly. If all this could happen to Noah, the righteous man, how much more is it a warning to the ordinary man!

On slander. A rabbi commanded his slave to buy the best food in the market. The slave brought home a tongue. The next day the rabbi commanded him to buy the worst food in the market, and once again, the slave brought home a tongue. When asked for an explanation, the wise slave answered, "There is nothing better than a good tongue, and nothing worse than an evil tongue."

On poverty. There is nothing worse than poverty. Certain of the wisest of the Jews said, "Put poverty in one scale, and all other sufferings in the other, and the two would balance." Others disagreed, saying, "The scales containing poverty would be even heavier."

On suffering. If a Jew breaks a leg, he says, "Praised be God that I did not break both legs"; if he breaks both, he says, "Praised be God that I did not break my neck."

When a man suffers tribulation, he should not say: "This is evil," for the Lord sends no evil. He should rather say: "I am undergoing a bitter experience." It is like a bitter medicine which a physician prescribes in order to cure the patient.

Rabbi Isaac Meyer lost every one of his thirteen sons. When the youngest died, the mother refused to be comforted. Her husband said to her, "Our sons have not died in vain. If a misfortune like ours should happen to another man, he will remember that we lost thirteen holy sons, and he will not feel angry against the Lord."

On the community. In the Torah, Jews are likened to sand. Each particle of sand is distinct, and only through fire do they become fused into glass. Likewise the Israelites are usually divided among themselves, and it requires calamities to unite them.

Israel is like a vine. A vine is trodden underfoot, but later its wine is placed on the table of the king. So, too, does Israel, at first oppressed, eventually come to greatness.

On family life. One man boasts of a son who was so loyal that when his father asked him for a drink of water and fell asleep, the son bent over him and stood there until his father awoke.

Anger in a home is like rottenness in fruit. Immorality in a home is like a worm in fruit.

On the role of women. Be careful about the honor of your wife, for blessing enters the house only because of the wife.

The emperor once said to Rabbi Gamaliel: "Your God is a thief, for did He not cause Adam to fall asleep and then steal one of his ribs?" Hearing this, the rabbi's daughter cried to the emperor to send for the police. The emperor responded,

"Why? What has happened?" The rabbi's daughter answered. "A robber entered my house last night and stole away a silver pitcher, but left a gold one in its place." The emperor said, "I wish such a thief would come to my house every night!" to which the rabbi's daughter shrewdly replied, "Why then do you accuse our God? Did he not steal a rib from Adam only to enrich him with a wife?"

Not all such writings are epigrams, anecdotes, or practical advice. A unique form of humor developed among the Jews, examples of which are found in the wisdom literature. This is called Yiddish humor.

Yiddish Humor

Because of their injustices and frustrations throughout history, the Jews developed a unique sense of humor as a defense against the insults leveled at them. Much of this humor was directed at themselves, as if self-inflicted insults robbed their assailants of victory. These witty stories transformed the Jew from the victim of mockery into its master. The examples included here fall into four categories: religious, schlemiels, schnorrers, and fools of Chelem.

Religious

To insulate the Jews from the insults of Christians who blamed the Jews for the death of Christ, some anecdotes pitted a priest and a rabbi against each other.

A Christian priest and a rabbi began arguing about the difference between belief in a God of love and belief in a God of vengeance. The rabbi claimed, "It is truth that we Jews believe in a God of vengeance, for it is written in the Bible, 'Vengeance is mine saith the Lord.' So we must leave vengeance to God. However, we must practice love toward our neighbor, for it is also written, 'Thou shalt love thy neighbor as thyself.' In your case, it is just the other way around. Now would you say that your Christian religion is the better religion?"

Sitting next to a rabbi at a banquet, a Christian priest decided to have some fun with him and offered him some spiced ham. "Thank you, Your Reverence," said the rabbi, "but don't you know such food is prohibited by my religion?"

"Oh?" responded the clergyman. "What a foolish religion. This ham is delicious."

When the banquet ended, the rabbi said goodby to the priest and added, "And please, Your Reverence, be so good as to pay my respects to your dear wife!"

"My wife?" he asked in horror. "Don't you know that my religion forbids me to marry?"

"Oh?" mused the rabbi. "What a foolish religion! A wife is so delicious!"

Schlemiels

A legendary folk hero, Motke Habad, is a classic schlemiel—an unlucky bungler, a Jew who is always trying to get ahead but never succeeds.

Motke Habad once became so desperate that he went to the heads of the village for help. "If you won't support me," Motke threatened, "I shall become a hatmaker!"

107

They laughed and countered, "So what if you do become a hatmaker?"

"Don't you see how serious this is?" argued Motke. "If I become a hatmaker, all the babies in the village will soon be born without heads!"

Motke once operated a horse-driven carriage, but soon discovered that he was spending all his profit on oats. So he decided to train his horse to eat oats one day less per week, then two, then three days less. After a month, the horse was down to two days a week when it suddenly collapsed and died.

Motke was grief-stricken. Standing over the dead horse, he was heard to complain, "Woe is me! Just when my troubles are almost over, you have to give up and die!"

Schnorrers

Another legendary character is the schnorrer, or professional panhandler. Unlike the schlemiel, who is stupid, the schnorrer is clever.

A rich man was relaxing in his home when he saw a schnorrer across the street scratching his back on a picket fence.

Acting surprised when the rich man came out, the schnorrer explained he had no money for a bath. The rich man gave him money for several baths, plus a change of clothes. When the news spread, two other beggars rushed to the same spot and began scratching themselves vigorously against the fence. Soon the rich man came out shouting angrily, "Get out of here, you imposters—you can't fool me!"

"But why," they asked, "did you believe the schnorrer?"

"Because he was alone and had to use the fence to scratch his back. But there are two of you and if you were not imposters, you'd scratch each other's back."

Fools of Chelem

When asked why the hair on a man's head turns gray sooner than his beard, a citizen of Chelem answered, "That's easy—the hair on a man's head is twenty years older than his beard."

Two fools of Chelem were taking a stroll when the first said, "The ways of heaven are mysterious. The birds are so small, eat so little, but have been given wings to go wherever they wish to get food. The cow is huge, needs much food, and moves about in one spot so slowly."

Just then, a flock of birds flew up and a speck landed on his nose. Wiping his nose with his sleeve, he continued, "I have solved the mystery!—I now know why the Lord in His wisdom didn't give wings to the cow!"

The Role of Women

Deeply rooted in the Jewish tradition is the "proverbial mother," often mentioned but seldom defined. Although exceptional Jewish women such as Golda Meir have assumed assertive leadership roles, Judaism has traditionally defined the woman's role as that of homemaker and mother, and these roles have been extolled by the Jews since ancient times. Hence the Jewish saying, "There is no bad mother, just as there is no good death." Although it is much less evident among liberal Jews, the male dominance of Judaism is preserved among the Orthodox.

Orthodox Jews often say, "A boy is a blessing; a girl is a worry." This attitude is evident in the treatment of children. Jewish boys often begin their school day at five in the morning and don't return home until eight in the evening. They often study in pairs, memorizing extended passages of Jewish law and tradition. Teen-age boys spend hours studying the Torah and the Talmud. Such complete dedication to the study of ancient Jewish writings might appear misdirected to an outsider who would think a broader study might be more useful in later life. If you would suggest this to an Orthodox Jew, however, he might reply by saying, "How unfortunate that great Jewish minds like Freud, Marx, and Einstein didn't concentrate on the Talmud—they would have been much better off." Jewish boys, sons of the covenant, receive rigorous training for leadership in the synagogue, the family, and the community.

Meanwhile, Jews do *not* encourage their daughters to study the Talmud. From their early years, Jewish girls learn the traditional practices required of an Orthodox housewife. Their lives revolve around their homes, as they learn to create orderly households and to attend to the many details related to Jewish holidays. Custom forbids a girl to shake hands with cousins, much less with gentiles, since she must present herself pure and unspoiled to her future husband. This may seem a far cry from sexual equality, but Jewish girls don't complain. They consider nothing more satisfying for a Jewish girl than to accept the Orthodox roles of mother and homemaker.

The circumstance of Israeli women is more extreme. The women of Israel are still second-class citizens, severely restricted by law and custom. For example, women are not allowed to testify in rabbinical courts, which handle divorce and marriage proceedings for all Jews. Wives cannot divorce without their husbands' permission, and widows without a male heir need the approval of a brother-in-law to remarry. If a woman has been widowed three times, all three husbands having died of natural causes, she is declared a "fatal woman" and is legally forbidden to marry again.

The restrictions placed on women are also evidenced by the limited number of career women in Israel. In civilian employment, only a third of Jewish women work outside the home, usually in low-paying jobs. Although the law requires equal pay for equal work, many women are paid less than men for similar tasks. Women are usually barred from work on the night shift since this is judged to be potentially harmful to their health.

Visitors to Israel report a resurgence of the feminine roles of mother, wife, and homemaker. To be single is considered the greatest misfortune a Jewish woman can experience. Perhaps the viewpoint of Jewish women is best expressed by the daughter of Moshe Dayan. During a visit with Betty Friedan, the American feminist, she revealed the state of women's liberation in Israel. Surrounded by her children, she reflected, "I presented myself a model of the slaving wife resigned to her fate."

Completed Jews

One of the great challenges confronting modern Judaism is focused on the person of Jesus Christ. Many rabbis urge Jews to be more open-minded about Christ. Other rabbis express concern for the increasing number of Jewish young people who are becoming messianic Christians and calling themselves "completed Jews." Let's examine these trends.

Until the mid-twentieth century, most Jews hated the very name of Jesus. Their hatred was not without cause, because Christians had taunted Jews for centuries, with insults such as "Christ-killers." Christians have generally condemned such warped anti-Semitism, acknowledging that all people share in the guilt of Christ's death, because it was for the sins of all that Christ died.

This new understanding has created a desire in the Jewish community to take another look at Jesus of Nazareth and, as one writer has put it, to take pride in Jesus the Jew. One prominent rabbi has challenged Jews to "Render unto Jesus that which is Jesus' " and to admit that His influence was beneficial to all people, Jew and gentile alike. According to newspaper reports, another rabbi recently stated publicly the belief that Jesus was raised by God from the dead. Yet the idea that Jesus was God in the flesh—Immanuel—is blasphemy to a devout Jew.

Accompanying this improved perception of Jesus, there is a growing concern among Jews over an evangelical Christian organization called "Jews for Jesus." Appealing primarily to young people, this group aggressively urges Jews to fulfill their Jewishness by accepting Jesus as the true Messiah. Sometimes called kosher Christians, these converts retain their Jewish culture and many of their Jewish practices, while accepting Jesus as their Messiah. Through newspaper ads and wide literature distribution, Jews for Jesus have irked many Jewish leaders who accuse them of proselytizing their youth. An estimated seven thousand people in the United States have become "completed Jews."

Questions

1. Read Philippians 3:4b–11. Explain how Paul regarded his Jewish heritage and his faith in Christ.
2. Read Matthew 23, in which Jesus denounces the teachers of the law and the Pharisees of His day. Then explain the words of Jesus that are found in Matthew 11:28–30.
3. Jewish leaders have been alarmed by the large number of Jewish young people who are attracted to the Jews for Jesus movement, as well as cults. What have you learned about Judaism that might explain this trend?
4. Christian groups such as the Moral Majority strongly support the Jewish state in its struggle to maintain its homeland. Do you agree or disagree with this position? Why?

For Further Study

1. Make a study of the Old Testament prophecies concerning the Jewish nation, and their fulfillment.
2. Study the work and character of the Zionist movement.
3. Report on contributions by Jews in the fields of art, science, and technology.
4. Study the Talmud and give examples of Jewish law and interpretation.
5. If you have a Jewish neighbor or friend, ask about the faith and practice of Judaism, and what being Jewish means personally.
6. Attend Orthodox, Reform, and Conservative Jewish services, and compare them.
7. Ask a local rabbi to talk to your class.
8. Read *The Chosen* by Chaim Potok and describe the religion of the Hasidic Jews in New York City.
9. Make a study of mission work done among the Jews by your denomination.
10. Discuss the way Christians should approach Jews with the gospel of Christ.
11. Study the Jewish sects of Christ's time—the Pharisees, the Sadducees, and the Essenes—and compare them with the three modern Jewish groups.

Additional Sources of Information

Books

Gross, David C. *One Thousand and One Questions and Answers about Judaism*. New York: Doubleday, 1978. Using the question-and-answer format, this book treats in ten chapters basic beliefs, customs and ceremonies, personal and family life, holidays and festivals, the synagogue, Israel, and Jewish history.

Pool, David De Sola. *Why I Am a Jew*. Boston: Beacon Press, 1957.

The author, a rabbi, tells what it means to be a Jew. This book covers most facets of Judaism and Jewish life.

Films

"The Chosen People," Time-Life, 1978.

Ronald Eyre takes the viewer to Jerusalem, where a rabbi serves as a guide through Jewish schools, a synagogue, and a museum for the survivors of the Holocaust. The film shows the Sabbath evening meal and other rituals. Part of television's "Long Search" series. Color. Fifty-two minutes. Also available in video.

Many films about Judaism are available for a low rental fee from the Jewish Community Council of Metropolitan Detroit, Fred M. Butzel Memorial Building, 163 Madison Avenue, Detroit, MI 48226. Jewish councils in other major cities should also have them.

Filmstrip

"The World's Great Religions: Judaism." Time-Life, 1957.

Portrays Jewish groups, teachings, scriptures, and observation of special days. Comes with lecture notes. Color.

5

Islam

The crescent-and-star symbol of Islam appears on the flags of several nations whose populations have Muslim majorities.

No religious creed is repeated more frequently than the Arabic phrase, "La Ilaha Illa Allah; Muhammad Rasul Allah." About 700 million Muslims—one out of every seven persons on earth—pause five times every day to proclaim this basic statement of faith which means, "There is no God but Allah; Muhammad is the Prophet of Allah." To call the followers of Islam "Muhammadans" is incorrect. The religion is named *Islam* (to surrender or submit); the follower is called *Muslim* (one who surrenders or submits); and the prophet who founded this religion was *Muhammad*. Since its founding in the seventh century, Islam has spread rapidly, spanning every race and all six continents. Today, Islam is winning ten times as many converts as Christianity in some emerging nations of Africa.

Historical Developments

The roots of Islam can be traced to early Arab society, where hundreds of tribes roamed the Arabian peninsula, a desert area of one million square

117

miles. Managing to survive in an especially hostile environment, the Arab (Arab means "nomad") tribes became fiercely competitive, often driven to bloody wars and long feuds. Their religion was polytheistic, with hundreds of gods and goddesses, all brought into being by the mother of gods, Allat. Powerful spirits in trees, mounds of earth, and stones influenced day-to-day existence positively, while powerful evil spirits or demons called *jinns* caused every kind of evil, from sores on a camel's hoof to tribal wars. Among these early Arabs, one god, Allah, was the supreme deity of all, but most of the nomads were attached to tribal gods far removed from him.

By the time Muhammad was born, religious devotion had weakened considerably. The uneducated nomads, having lost faith in their gods, had turned to other religious practices to discover the secrets of life and the future. Some became astrologers, scanning the signs and secrets of the planets to determine their destiny. Others turned to the practice of dissecting birds and mice and examining the livers to find omens for good or bad fortune. Still others followed the ancient practice of casting lots, exploring magical formulas by which the secrets of the gods could be learned.

With the decline of religious devotion came widespread social evils. Drawing lots led to gambling; gambling led to other degrading activities. The Arabs earned a reputation for brawling, excessive drinking, and sexual promiscuity. Jews and Christians who came to Arabia preached a nobler way of life. They preached a code of morals which brought personal peace and social order, and taught the Arabs about the one God, who resembled Allah. The Arabs rejected both the Christian and the Jewish teachings. But among them was one who did listen—Muhammad.

Muhammad's Life

Most of the details of Muhammad's life were not recorded until years after his death, but the basic story is well known. Born into the Quraysh tribe around the year 570, Muhammad (meaning "highly praised") was orphaned at an early age and reared by an uncle, Abu Talib, who became his adoptive father. As a boy, Muhammad worked on camel caravans, often traveling to trade centers of the Middle East. Here he came into contact with Christians and Jews and listened intently to their discussions of monotheism and morals. Muhammad was a sensitive lad, repulsed by the immorality of his own people, which often caused him to experience times of depressed brooding.

By his early twenties, Muhammad was an attractive man, with a massive chest, a handsome face, and a prominent nose. (People said his nose drank before his mouth.) Muhammad was also popular. At the age of twenty-five, he married Khadijah, a forty-year-old widow who owned a flourishing caravan business. With his financial security assured by Khadijah's wealth, Muhammad began to venture into the desert to contemplate and pray, as had other Arab holy men before him. Over the years, he made periodic visits to a cave on Mount Hira, just three miles from his home. His vigils of meditation sometimes lasted many hours, perhaps several days, and his wife became worried for his physical and emotional well-being.

One night in the year 610, when Muhammad was about forty, the Muslim faith began. In the cave where he had spent six months in solitary meditation, Muhammad received a vision. The angel Gabriel roused him with the stern command, "Proclaim!" Not knowing whether this was a dream or a vision, Muhammad responded, "But what shall I proclaim? I cannot read!" Suddenly his throat tightened as though the angel were choking him. Again came the command: "Proclaim!" And again Muhammad protested, "I cannot read," only to feel the choking grip again and hear the third command:

Proclaim in the Name of the Lord,
The Creator who created man from a clot of
    blood!
Proclaim. Your Lord is most gracious,
Who has taught by the pen
What man did not know. [Koran, chap. 46:1-4]

When the vision had ended, Muhammad found the experience and the exact words of the angel "engraved on his heart," and he could neither understand what they meant not trust the validity of his vision. Had it been only a dream? What did it mean? Had evil spirits invaded him? These unanswered questions depressed him so severely that he contemplated suicide. But just as he was about to take his life, an unidentified force prevented him. Trembling with fright, he heard the voice again, "I am Gabriel, the angel of Allah, and you Muhammad are the prophet of Allah." From that day on Muhammad believed that he was Allah's prophet to the Arabs.

Muhammad began preaching immediately and his wife became his first convert. New revelations came very gradually, sometimes separated by many months, and as they came, Muhammad preached the new faith of Islam. Some of this religion was familiar to Arabs who knew about the monotheism of the Jews and Christians. They could readily accept Muhammad's claim, for example, that Allah, long regarded as the highest of the desert gods, was the same God that was worshiped by Jews and Christians. But opposition grew. Other Arabs felt threatened by Muhammad's growing power, and Jews and Christians questioned his claim that he was revealing the true word of God to the Arabs. Having long been "People of the Book," the Jews privately wondered whether Muhammad was conjuring up revelations so that the Arabs could also become "People of the Book." After twelve years of unproductive preaching, and harassment by opponents, Muhammad and his followers escaped to Medina in 622, in a migration known as the *hegira*. This night, called The Night of the Flight, marks year one on the Muslim calendar.

To a growing number of believers, Muhammad began to elaborate on his new religion. Revelations came to him during trances; his descriptions of those encounters, memorized and recorded by his adherents, were later collected to comprise the Muslim sacred book, the Koran

(Qur'an, in Arabia). As his followers grew in strength and number, Muhammad began a series of raids on Meccan caravans, which led to several indecisive battles with their avenging war parties. In 628, the Meccans agreed to let Muhammad's followers make their pilgrimage to the Kaaba, which the new religion regarded as a sacred shrine. Two years later, the prophet led an army of 10,000 into his former city, taking control in a bloodless victory.

Despite the legends that developed, beginning already during his lifetime, Muhammad remained a humble man who rejected any claim to deity, insisting that he was merely the human conduit of Allah. He occasionally incurred the wrath of his wives and concubines. All of his sons died in childhood, leaving him without a male heir. In 632 he led a pilgrimage to Mecca where he declared, "I have perfected your religion and completed my favors for you." Three months later he fell ill in Medina and died. His final words, it is reported, were a prayer, "O Allah, pardon my sins. . . ." To his zealous followers went the task of spreading the word of Allah, not only throughout Arabia, but far beyond as well. Let's examine the basic beliefs taught by Muhammad and preserved for the past 1,300 years in Islam.

Muslim Beliefs

The Koran

The core of Islam is contained within the holy book of Islam, the Koran, which means "the reciting" or "the reading." It is four-fifths the size of the New Testament, and millions of Muslims have succeeded in memorizing it word for word. Each chapter of the Koran, it is believed, relates a revelation which Muhammad received through the angel Gabriel during a period of twenty-two years. Orthodox Muslims accept the Koran (only in Arabic) as divinely inspired. They believe Allah preserved its literal accuracy and caused it to be a perfect copy, word for word, of the original Koran, which exists in heaven.

The teachings of the Koran are found in 114 chapters, almost exactly in order of decreasing length. However, three passages of the Koran stand out as representative of the entire book.

His peers, the Koreish, asked Muhammad to name the attributes of Allah. His answer, chapter 112, is held in particular veneration and is declared to be equal in value to a third of the whole Koran: "Say, God is one God; the eternal God: he begetteth not, neither is he begotten and there is not any one like unto him" (chap. 62).

Islam reveres the opening chapter of the Koran as the quintessence of the faith, which means that the purest, most concentrated truth of Islam is contained here. This opening chapter is often called The Lord's Prayer of Islam: "In the name of God, Most Gracious, Most Merciful. Praise be to God, the Cherisher and Sustainer of the Worlds; Most Gracious, Most Merciful; Master of the Day of Judgment. Thee do we worship, and Thine aid we seek. Show us the straight way, the way of those on whom Thou hast bestowed Thy Grace, those whose [portion] is not wrath, and who go not astray" (chap. 1).

The brief passage which is commonly called the Apostles' Creed of Islam appears on many of the mosques or places of prayer. "God! There is no God but He—the Living, the Self-subsisting, Eternal. No slumber can seize Him, nor sleep. His are all things in the heavens and on earth. Who is there that can intercede in His presence except as He permitteth? He knoweth what [appeareth to His creatures as] Before or After or Behind them. Nor shall they compass aught of His knowledge except as He willeth. His Throne doth extend over the heavens and the earth, and He feeleth no fatigue in guarding and preserving them" (chap. 2:256).

The theme of these three passages is, of course, the omnipotence (total power) of Allah. Other themes occurring in the Koran are the inevitability of the day of judgment, the horrors of hell, and the bliss of heaven.

Ranking beneath the Koran in value, but of considerable religious significance, the *Hadith* is a collection of the alleged sayings, teachings, rulings, and deeds of the prophet Muhammad, compiled by scholars about two hundred years after his death. The Hadith provides the Muslim with details of the life of Muhammad, who was regarded as the perfect Muslim, so the believer can imitate him.

Five Articles of Faith

Every Muslim accepts five primary doctrines:

1. belief in Allah as the one true God

2. belief in angels as the instruments or messengers of Allah
3. belief in four inspired books, of which the Koran is the final and most complete
4. belief in twenty-eight prophets of Allah, of whom Muhammad is the last
5. belief in a final day of judgment

Let's examine each of these articles of faith in greater detail.

Belief in Allah as the one true God. From high in the *minaret* (a high tower), the holy men of Islam call out five times a day, "La Ilaha Illa Allah; Muhammad Rasul Allah." This is the *Shahada*, which means, "There is no God but Allah; Muhammad is the Prophet of Allah." Muslims strongly believe Allah to be the one, eternal, all-powerful creator who has no rival and shares his glory with no other creature. One of the most serious sins, according to Islam, is the sin of *shirk*, ascribing glory to someone other than Allah. Christian belief in Jesus as the begotten Son of God is considered shirk because, Muslims believe, it detracts from the glory of Allah and divides the absolute unity of Allah.

Muslims believe that Allah is omniscient (all-knowing), omnipresent (everywhere present), immutable (unchanging), and infinite (free from all limitations). Tradition teaches ninety-nine titles of praise for Allah, including The Holy, The Shelterer of Orphans, The Friend of the Bereaved, The Deliverer, The Merciful, and The Generous. An interesting Islamic legend claims there is a hundredth name, but only the camel knows what it is, which explains why the camel is haughty. Many

Muslims use a rosary of ninety-nine beads for reciting the names of Allah.

Christians often point out that Islam lacks the name used frequently by Jesus—God the Father. Samuel Zwemer, lifelong missionary to the Muslims, notes, "The Koran shows that Muhammad had a measurably correct idea of the spiritual attributes of God, but an absolutely false conception of his moral attributes. The conception of God is negative. Absolute Sovereignty and ruthless omnipotence are his chief attributes, while His character is impersonal. . . . [1] Perhaps this explains why prayers of petition are not prominent in Islam, for Islam conceives of Allah in terms of the will, not in terms of moral attributes such as goodness, mercy, grace, love, long-suffering, or patience.

Everyday language in Muslim countries contains countless reminders of Islam's belief that nothing on earth happens without Allah's will. Tell a Cairo taxi driver where you want to go, and he will answer, "Inshallah" ("If Allah wills"). If a housewife finds fresh fruit in the marketplace, she might whisper, "Al-hamdulillah" ("Praise be to Allah"). As the farmer sows his field, he will repeat, "Bismillah" ("In the name of Allah").

A bit of recent history was influenced by the Islamic emphasis on the will of Allah. The world took note when the late president of Egypt, Anwar Sadat, a devout Muslim, made his historic trip to Jerusalem in search of peace with Israel. Sadat

1. *Islam: A Challenge to Faith* (New York: Student Volunteer Movement for Foreign Missions, 1907).

knew that Allah controlled every detail, however small, of his mission. He kept repeating quietly, "This is my fate, and I accept my fate, whatever the outcome."

Belief in angels as messengers of Allah. Frequently mentioned in the Koran, angels are messengers of Allah, constantly ready to do the will of Allah. They worship Allah continually, hold up his throne, descend to earth from time to time with his decrees, keep records of each person's behavior, and receive the souls of people who die. Angels frequently encouraged the prophets of Allah, just as Gabriel instructed and encouraged Muhammad. In addition to the good angels, the Muslim recognizes fallen, evil angels called jinns, who have an evil influence. Bad crops, high prices, and food shortages are routinely attributed to the influence of jinns.

Belief in four inspired scriptures. Islam accepts three sets of scriptures as revelations of Allah's will: the Torah of Moses, the Psalms of David, and the gospel of Jesus. However, these are *partial* revelations which contain errors of translation and historical fact. Only the Koran represents the final and complete revelation, superseding all prior scriptures. The others contain truth, but the Koran contains the whole and final truth. And the Koran, unlike the others, contains a message for all people.

Belief in twenty-eight prophets of Allah. Muslims believe that Allah revealed his message to humankind over a long period of time, using prophets as messengers or conduits. Two classes of prophets were selected by Allah: those who introduced new teachings and those who merely repeated the messages of earlier prophets. The first and most important were Adam, Noah, Abraham, Moses, Jesus, and Muhammad, in that order. Others, such as Ishmael, Joseph, David, Job, and John the Baptist were of the second category. Most of the prophets are Bible characters but the non-biblical Alexander the Great is also considered a prophet.

Not only is Muhammad considered the most important prophet, but also many zealous Muslims have idealized him as the most perfect human being who ever lived. Revelations to earlier prophets were incomplete; and disobedient, stubborn people often distorted their messages. So it was to the last and greatest prophet that the complete truth of Allah, in pure form, was revealed. Other more educated Muslims readily concede that Muhammad never claimed perfection, nor did he regard himself as a miracle worker, but he was, they insist, the last and greatest, the "seal" of the lineage of Allah's prophets.

Belief in a final day of judgment. Common to Jews, Christians, and Muslims is belief in a day of judgment. Christians are usually surprised to learn that Islam teaches the return of Jesus to the earth. Sometime before the final day of judgment, Muslims believe, Jesus will rule in Jerusalem for a period of forty years, after which He will die and be buried beside the body of Muhammad at Medina. They believe that a vacant tomb is kept in readiness. Presumably this forty-year rule will provide Christians with an opportunity to attain salvation with the Muslims. Then the day of judgment will come.

The details of the day of judgment are set forth in the Koran. After many signs in the heavens, a trumpet blast will call forth the dead in a general resurrection. Everyone, living and dead, will gather on a great plan and receive the book containing a record of their thoughts and deeds. If the book is delivered to the right hand, the reward of heaven will provide luxurious opportunity to read the book, as described in the Koran: "A banquet of fruits, and honoured shall they be, In the gardens of delight, upon couches face to face. A cup shall be borne round among them from a fountain; limpid, delicious to those who drink: It shall not oppress the sense, nor shall they therewith be drunken. And with them are the large-eyed ones with modest, refraining glances. . . . Truly great is their felicity!" (chap. 37). Other descriptions of heaven tell of perpetual luxury, physical comfort, abundant food, clear water, and lovely maidens for the righteous.

Descriptions of hell are equally vivid. If the book of deeds is delivered to the left hand, the condemned sinner will respond, "Would that I had not been given my book and not known by reckoning; Would it had been the end! My wealth has not availed me . . ." (chap. 69). Unbelievers and greedy, selfish sinners will experience boiling liquids, molten metal, and putrid smells, as portrayed in this quotation from the Koran: "Behold, he never believed in God the All-mighty, and he never urged the feeding of the needy; therefore he has not here one loyal friend, neither any food saving foul pus, that none excepting the sinners eat" (chap. 69).

Every device is employed to prevent a loved one from going to hell, including a common funeral practice among Muslims. Muhammad taught that when a Muslim dies and his body is buried, two angels visit the corpse. Ordering the body to sit up, they ask:

Who is your God?
Who is your Prophet?
What is your faith?
Which is your book?
Where is your kiblah?[2] [chap. 37]

To assure that every Muslim remembers, the funeral includes advice to the deceased, "O Son of Adam, when the two angels come to question you, answer them, 'God, greatest in glory is my only Lord; Muhammad, my Prophet; Islam, my faith; the Koran, my book; and the Holy House at Mecca, my kiblah.' " If these answers are given, the two angels leave the dead Muslim in peace until the final resurrection.

The way of salvation

The words *Islam* and *Muslim*, as we have seen, offer a clue for the lifestyle required of a devout Muslim. The greatest virtue, complete submission to the will and authority of Allah, must be practiced. The moral precepts set forth in the Koran include five specific duties known as the Five Pillars, which must be observed if one wishes to enter heaven.

2. *Kiblah* means "holy city."

First pillar: the Shahada. The first words spoken into the ear of a Muslim baby and the last uttered over the corpse at the grave are, the profession of faith: "There is no God but Allah; Muhammad is the Prophet of Allah." The Shahada is similar to what Christians might call a testimony or profession of faith. A person may become a member of Islam after repeating the Shahada publicly, fervently, and with absolute conviction.

Second pillar: prayer. In Islam, prayer is called the "key to paradise," the most important duty. Each sincere prayer is intended to praise and thank Allah, to remind worshipers of their inferiority, and to teach humility. Some prefer to call this worship because of the emphasis on reverence, instead of prayer, which normally includes supplications or requests. Most certainly the mood of reverence and awe pervades in the Muslim's experience of prayer.

Five times every day—at daybreak, at noon, in the midafternoon, after sunset, and before retiring—the *imam* (holy man) climbs to the minaret and leads the faithful in prayer. Wherever they may be and whatever they may be doing, the faithful drop everything for prayer. Muslims pray in a mosque at least once a week—Friday at noon. Other times they pray wherever they happen to be—at a shopping mall, in a parking lot, at school, at home, or at a ball diamond. For added incentive in the early morning, the *muezzin* (who announces the time for prayer) usually adds, "Prayer is better than sleep."

Prayer also includes proper preparation. Before Muslims begin to pray, they must purify themselves by washing all exposed parts of the body. Water from any source is acceptable and if no water is available, sand may be used instead. The hands are washed three times, the mouth is rinsed three times, then the elbows, arms, hands, face, ears, back of the neck, feet, and toes are washed. Special ritual words accompany each washing, and in conclusion, the person looks down at the ground and says, "I testify there is no God but Allah, Muhammad is the Apostle of Allah." These washings purify physically as prayer is believed to cleanse spiritually, so that the believer is completely pure in the sight of Allah. The washing completed, Muslims cover their heads, remove their shoes, and face the direction of the Kaaba in Mecca.

Once preparations are completed, the Muslim worshiper bows to the ground in a series of seven movements interspersed with prayers of devotion such as, "God is most Great," "Great God," and "Allah the Highest." The sight of worshipers lined up in rows, reciting the prayers in unison while their foreheads touch the ground, has caused many observers to admire the deep devotion, reverence, and piety of the Muslim at prayer.

Third pillar: giving alms. Once warning that a man who doesn't give alms will have a serpent twisted about his neck at the resurrection, Muhammad established the great importance of charity. In several Islamic states today, an annual tax of 2.5 percent is levied against an individual's assets (not income) for the benefit of the poor and needy. Those to whom Allah has given in abundance must share their good fortune. The good

Muslim must never refuse the beggar who asks for help "in the name of Allah." Alms are encouraged by the Koran, which claims that alms given to the poor in secret have power to atone for sins. Another implication of this pillar prohibits charging interest, especially to the poor and disadvantaged. Islamic banks today do not charge interest, but take equity in the projects they finance, sharing in losses as well as profits.

Fourth pillar: fasting. If prayer is called the "key to paradise," fasting might well be called the "gate to paradise." Except for the ill, every Muslim over age fourteen is expected to fast during the month of Ramadan, the ninth month of the year on Islam's lunar calendar. For the entire month, each Muslim must abstain from smoking, drinking, inhaling perfume, bathing, and having sexual intercourse from predawn until sunset; the truly devout even strive to avoid swallowing their saliva. When the fasting becomes difficult, one remembers the generations-old advice, "You can't please God without fasting!"

The value of fasting is tied to the central idea of surrender. By denying physical desires, the spirit focuses on the glory of Allah. As the will exerts strict self-discipline, one remembers the need to submit also to the will of Allah. A strong sense of religious duty and humble dependence results from the thirty-day fast. The fast also reminds one of the hunger of the poor and inspires almsgiving. The Koran sums up the purpose of fasting, teaching that the fast was ordained in order that the faithful might fear Allah.

Fifth pillar: pilgrimage. The fifth pillar of Islam

is *hajj*, or pilgrimage. A Muslim saying claims that if one dies without having visited the Holy House at Mecca, one might just as well have died a Jew or a Christian. So every devout Muslim attempts to make at least one pilgrimage to Mecca, an accomplishment which earns pilgrims the title of *hajji* before their names and promises them special consideration on the day of judgment.

During the hajj, pilgrims throng to Mecca, the men dressed in two seamless cotton cloths about the size of bath towels, and the women in white head-to-toe costumes, complete with veils. Pilgrims walk seven times around the Kaaba, a cubical stone building with a gold-embroidered black covering, which houses the famous Black Stone. Entering the empty Kaaba, pilgrims recall Muhammad's destruction of all the idols once kept there. Pilgrims also visit other holy sites, act out the search for water by Hagar, perform a vigil on the mountain where Muhammad preached his last sermon, and conduct a ritual sacrifice of goats, sheep, and camels.

Muslim Lifestyle

Shari'a

During the past thirteen centuries, Islamic scholars and religious leaders have compiled an all-embracing code of ethics, morality, and criminal and civil law called the *Shari'a*. Based on the

Koran, the life of Muhammad, and the agreement of Islamic leaders, the Shari'a must be observed by devout believers. Some of its laws seem unreasonably cruel. Note for example, the following provisions of Shari'a:

Adulterers are either scourged or stoned.

A Muslim caught drinking alcohol is given eight lashes.

A thief is punished by having a hand cut off.

Women must dress modestly, not exposing their skin in public.

A husband can divorce his wife by saying "I divorce you" three times in front of witnesses.

Women may receive a very limited inheritance, only a small fraction of that given to men.

Falsely accusing a woman of loose behavior (adultery) calls for a public flogging.

Other precepts of the path are simple instructions for practical living: pork is forbidden, gambling is condemned, astrology is outlawed, parents must not be neglected.

Muslims strongly defend the Shari'a against charges of cruelty. First of all, they point out, a thief can lose his hand only if he steals in a "just society," not if he is driven by hunger; and a woman can be convicted of adultery only if four eyewitnesses can be found. Also, in many Islamic societies, Muslims pridefully cite statistics for crime and violence which are much lower than those of most countries. Finally, Muslims point out that very tough laws and penalties for possession of drugs in the United States seem unreasonably cruel to them, more cruel perhaps than a public flogging. Reflecting on these explanations, most people modify their criticism of the Shari'a as unreasonably cruel.

As we shall note, the return to the Shari'a in the modern Islamic world has caused confusion and political instability. As Islamic republics have become more aggressive in today's world, the importance of the Shari'a has increased dramatically.

The Role of Women

Over the years, the Muslim world has earned a reputation for restricting the rights of women. According to long-standing Muslim traditions, women receive only one-half the inheritance that male heirs receive. And in a court of law, the testimony of two females is needed to match the value of one male witness's testimony. Until the twentieth century, education was reserved for males; women were regarded basically as homemakers and mothers. Divorce laws traditionally favored the husband and, as a result, the woman often sought security by having many sons who could support her if her husband divorced her. The inferior status held by women in the past was largely due to custom but also arose, in part, from a Muslim interpretation of the Koran. Even today, traditional Muslim women appear in public wearing the *chuddar*, a floor-length gown that leaves only the face exposed. In private, a wife is required by custom to remain in the background, forbidden to eat at the table with her husband when his invited guests are present.

While the Koran expressly states that Allah makes no distinctions between people on the basis of class, race, nationality, or sex, some passages might also be interpreted to discriminate against women. For example, the Koran teaches that women should be treated equally, even though men are a degree above them. The Koran also teaches that Allah does not prefer one sex to another, but offers this rationale: Allah has merely made one sex to excel over the other! In summary, the Koran teaches that men are superior to women by nature, more powerful and capable of confronting the struggles of life.

During the twentieth century, however, Muslim women began to assert themselves, demanding more equal treatment in marriage, careers, and society. As industrialization and progress influenced their countries, women increasingly sought liberation from the roles of housewife and mother. The education of Muslim women provides dramatic evidence of this change. In 1928, Cairo University enrolled its first five females— secretly, during the summer vacation, to prevent a male uproar. Today, forty-two percent of Cairo University's 130,000 students are female. Led by progressive women like the wife of the late President Sadat, Muslim women campaigned for equal rights under the slogan, "Only in weak societies are women weak."[3] As a result, the Muslim coun-

3. For a detailed treatment of feminism in Muslim countries, see the *New York Times Magazine*, March 16; 1980.

tries of Tunisia, Egypt, and Iran passed laws granting equal rights to women. However, the resurgence of conservative Islam has reversed the advances of feminist Muslim groups in some countries.

Beginning with the fanatic exhortations of Iran's Ayatollah Khomeini, a zealous wave of antifeminism swept across the Muslim world. In Tunisia, for example, students belonging to a group called the Muslim Brothers painted verses from the Koran over sexually suggestive billboard advertisements as part of their war "against sin and evil." Hundreds of female students at Cairo University have donned the veil and demanded classes separate from male students. But nowhere has the changing role of women been seen more vividly than in Iran.

On the Iranian coast of the Caspian Sea, at a beach resort once called the "Iranian Riviera," fences jut out from the beaches far into the water because Khomeini forbade men and women to swim together. In the beach areas, unmarried couples holding hands or showing physical affection were sought out by religious zealots and ordered to behave. By an edict from Khomeini, all music was banned from Iran's radio stations during the month of Ramadan. Television shows, including "Kojak" and "Wonder Woman," were removed from the air due to their immorality and perverted portrayal of women. One visitor to Iran reported that two teen-age girls who were observed giggling at a hotel swimming pool were arrested for immodest and immoral behavior. Once again, in Muslim countries where Shi'ite

Muslims have regained control, women wear the chuddar and resume the traditional and passive role. Still, resentment continues to smolder among Muslim feminists.

Whether conservative or progressive, all Muslims look upon marriage as one of the most important of all institutions. Great emphasis is placed on the religious and social value of a close-knit family life. Although it remains true that a Muslim male is allowed as many as four wives, polygamy is practiced by less than four percent of the population. The Koran permits taking additional wives only in special circumstances, such as when a widow has no means of support or a wife becomes physically or mentally incapacitated. If a husband has more than one wife, he is legally required to treat them all equally.

Islam Today

For many centuries after its first century of spectacular expansion, Islam tended to keep a low profile, to be conservative and complacent. Missionary expansion seemed less important than scrupulous obedience to the truths which had been revealed. Then, in the nineteenth century, a famous religious leader, Mohammad Abduh, began to provide dynamic leadership.

Mohammad Abduh attacked conservatism and called for modernization. Education, he contended, must be expanded to prepare people for the age of technology. If Islam did not change, he warned, the values of Western industry, science, and social stability would be denied the Muslim countries. As a result, Islamic society began to change. Progressive Muslims worked toward greater equality for women, improved education, industrial growth, and modernization of their cities. This progress has continued far into the twentieth century.

The month Ramadan was chosen for fasting because important historical events occurred during this month. The first revelation received by Muhammad came during Ramadan in 610. The historic flight from Mecca to Medina also occurred in that month. And a famous battle at Badr—a do-or-die battle for the struggling early followers of Muhammad—was fought during Ramadan. Combined with these historical meanings, the fast during Ramadan becomes a rallying point among Muslims throughout the world, bringing strong feelings of unity and brotherhood.

Ramadan, however, is not a month to be dreaded by the Muslim family, a fact which helps to explain why a North American motel chain chose the name of "Ramada Inns." At the end of each day's fast, families gather to "break the fast," which is done in safe stages. They first sip a cool drink, then a cup of tea or soda pop. Then they pass trays of nuts and fruit and nibble on appetizers. Soon they light their pipes, and the families sit down for a meal, followed by games, music, and dancing. At the end of the month there are lavish celebrations—dancing in the streets and feasting in the homes. When Ramadan falls in the hot summer months, the daylight hours of fasting are long and the fast is severe.

Along with modernization came lifestyles and Western values which eroded the principles cherished in the Shari'a. Health clinics and improved health care reduced disease and extended life expectancy, but also aggravated the expanding problem of overpopulation and strained the ability to feed the masses. Rapid growth of industry provided jobs, but family structures broke down as fathers and husbands were lured to the cities in search of wealth. Western television programs brought entertainment to the country—"Happy Days," "Charlie's Angels," and "Laverne and Shirley"—but these programs encouraged easy lifestyles, lowered moral standards, and suggested frivolous attitudes toward self-discipline. In short, the Western lifestyle of self-gratification and self-indulgence directly opposed the submission and humble dependence inherent in Islam.

Repelled by the bitter fruits of modernization, or perhaps Westernization, Muslims are rediscovering their spiritual roots. The revival of Islam, gaining strength over several decades, has been felt throughout the Middle East. Iran provides the most telling example. After deposing the Shah—a symbol of Westernization—the people went to the polls and voted in the nation's first "government of God," led by Ayatollah Khomeini. Soon after the Shari'a was enforced as the law of the land in the new Islamic republic, strict retributive justice to the "friends of the Shah" accompanied a closing of bars, gambling casinos, liquor factories, and pornography shops. The rule of Khomeini was hailed by one Muslim magazine: "The Muslims are coming, despite Jewish cunning, Christian hatred, and the communist storm." Muslims the world over reflect the same objection: they want to obtain the technology, the agricultural techniques, and the fruits of modernization, but they reject the evils associated with modernization—lowered moral standards, secular lifestyles, and the breakdown of family structure. Cyrus Vance, formerly American secretary of state, correctly observed, "The Islamic resurgence in a number of countries indicates a return to fundamental roots and a greater reliance on principles that were pushed aside in the move toward modernization."

Rediscovery of their spiritual heritage has made the Muslims evangelistic. In the current competition for converts in Africa, Islam holds three distinct advantages over Christianity. The Islamic toleration of polygamy, for example, is welcomed by African tribes where polygamy has been a way of life. Islam also stresses the brotherhood of humanity and has welcomed blacks as equals with no apparent racism or paternalism like that which the Christian Church has often imposed. In addition, all Muslims, whether merchants, tourists, or diplomats, consider themselves missionaries, responsible for spreading the true faith of Islam. Clearly these factors provide helpful contacts in Muslim missionary efforts.

The number of Muslims throughout the world is second only to the number of Christians, and it continues to increase in parts of the world. There are more than fifteen countries in northern Africa and southern Asia where almost everyone is a

Muslim. Since there are almost no native Christians in these countries, converts to Christianity are viewed as backsliders. Also, ninety percent or more of the people in Egypt, Kuwait, Syria, Iraq, Iran, Afghanistan, and Indonesia are Muslim. Christians are a persecuted minority in Islamic countries.

The growth of Islam can be explained in part by high birth rates. Other factors in its growth are immigration and missionary work, especially in central and southern Africa, Europe, and North America. Nigeria and Chad are about one-half Muslim. England and the Netherlands have received Muslim immigrants from former colonies. Muslim people from Morocco, Algeria, Tunisia, and Libya go to France because it is nearby and because they can speak French. They also go to Montreal, where there is a large Muslim community. Another is in Dearborn, Michigan. Mission work in the United States is done by Muslim immigrants and by the Black Muslims, who say that Christianity is for white people and Islam is for black people. Mission work in the United States and Canada is supported by Saudi Arabia. But since the Muslim people who come to North America are free to choose what they believe, Christian people can also be active missionaries among them here.

As a major religion of the Eastern world, Islam must be recognized as a highly influential and rapidly expanding system of belief and lifestyle with tremendous power to affect and direct individuals, political systems, and entire countries.

Questions

1. Today there is a return of the Muslims to the Koran and to the Koranic culture of early Islam. Give examples from recent history in Iran and other Middle Eastern countries to illustrate this.
2. Do the Muslims believe in the same God that we do?
3. Is the conflict between the Arab Muslims and Israel in any way a religious conflict?
4. Examine the Black Muslim movement in the United States. How has it moved closer to Islam in recent years?
5. The Koran teaches that Jesus was never crucified. Muslims say that the man on the cross was someone else. How do you know that Jesus was indeed the man on the cross?
6. Read a Muslim account of the way Muhammad received his first vision. How do you explain what happened?

For Further Study

1. After studying II Timothy 3:16 and II Peter 1:21, compare the Christian and Islamic meanings of inspiration. Is the Bible inspired in the same sense as the Muslims believe the Koran is inspired? Why or why not?
2. The first seventy years of Islam were years of tremendous growth. Some scholars have pointed out that Islam grew by force, not by true conversions. Research the way Islam grew and expanded in those early years and contrast this with the spread of Christianity.
3. When Muhammad first went to Medina, many residents there were Jews or Christians. At first Muhammad required Muslims to face Jerusalem when they

prayed. Why do you think he did that? Can you offer some explanation for his later persecution of Jews and the change of direction for prayer from Jerusalem to Mecca?

4. Islam is an all-encompassing way of life—a world-and-life view. There's no such thing as a religious compartment; religion is the life and life the religion. Is this also true of Christianity? In what specific ways ought Christians to shape and influence legal systems, political parties, or civil laws?

5. Many examples of the current resurgence of Islam can be found in newspapers and magazines. Cut out examples which indicate how the Shari'a is being restored in Islamic countries.

6. When the Black Muslims became established in the United States, the Islamic faith rejected them as followers of a new heresy. More recently the Black Muslims name has been changed from "Black Muslims" to "World Community of Islam in the West" and they are accepted by Islam as part of the true faith. Explore the changes in belief that caused this acceptance.

7. Name instances or situations where racism and lack of acceptance of other ethnic groups has hindered the missionary work of the Christian church.

Additional Sources of Information

Books

Kelen, Betty. *Muhammad: The Messenger of God*. New York: Elsevier–Nelson, 1975.
An objective account of the life of Muhammad, including his teachings and the culture of his times.

Pickthall, Marmaduke William. *The Meaning of the Glorious Koran*. London: Allen and Unwin, 1957.
This is one of the best and most readable translations of the Koran.

Wilson, J. Christy. *Introducing Islam*. Revised edition. New York: Friendship, 1957.
A well-written and attractive study of Islam from a Christian perspective.

Films

"Islam, the Prophet and the People." Texture Films, 1975.
An award-winning film showing the history of Islam and the basic beliefs of Muslims today. Color. Thirty-four minutes.

"There Is No God but God." Time-Life, 1978.
In this film, Ronald Eyre travels to Egypt to explore the Islamic experience. He visits a mosque in Cairo and interviews its sheikh. He witnesses a wedding in a small Egyptian rural community and follows Muslim pilgrims on their way to Mecca. Part of television's "Long Search" series. Color. Fifty-two minutes. Also available in video.

Filmstrip

"The World's Great Religions: Islam." Time-Life, 1957.
Portrays the origin, teachings, and practices of Islam. Comes with lecture notes. Color.

6

Summary

This study of world religions has been based on the biblical premise that God has written something about Himself in the hearts of all people. This fact explains the sincere piety, deep reverence, and impressive wisdom of many non-Christian religious traditions. The Muslim's acceptance of Christian Scriptures, the Jew's close relationship with a loving and faithful Jehovah, the Hindu's yearning to reunite with the Supreme Being, the Buddhist's denial of the value of earthly possessions and desires—all these things result from God's revelation to all humanity.

But at the same time that we recognize right responses to the human need to praise and return to God, we must recognize that non-Christian religions fail at the crucial point of belief in Jesus Christ, who said, "No one comes to the Father, but by me" (John 14:6).

Table 1 is included to help you review the elements of each religion covered in this book.

Table 1

Religion	Origin and Location	Beliefs The Supreme Being
Hinduism	The roots of Hinduism lie in the highly animistic, polytheistic religion of tribes who migrated to the Indus Valley, bringing their scriptures, the Vedas, and their social system, the caste system. There are presently about 450 million Hindus. Three-fourths live in India. Most others live in countries near India. Hinduism is diverse, often called a fellowship or museum of faiths.	Hinduism has assimilated 330 million gods. The most prominent gods are Brahma, Vishnu, and Shiva. Krishna was a loving, compassionate incarnation of the Supreme Being. Each Hindu is free to believe in a favorite god or gods.
Buddhism	Siddhartha Gautama (b. 565 B.C.), a Hindu prince, left his lavish life to search for truth. On his thirty-fifth birthday, he solved the mysteries of the universe and became Buddha. Buddhism is based in eastern and central Asia. Athough Gautama rejected many Hindu teachings, the influence of Hinduism is clear.	Gautama ignored the question of a divine being. He taught that speculation about matters of faith was wasteful, and time was better spent helping people with the realities of present life. Ironically, Buddhists have developed complicated forms of worship and deified Buddha himself.

Beliefs		Scriptures
The Human Predicament	**The Way of Salvation**	**Distinctive Practices**
Each human being is like a drop of World Soul, separated from this Cosmic Force and trapped in the dreaded cycle of birth and rebirth. The only way to escape this cycle is to work toward union once again with World Soul (nirvana).	To achieve nirvana, one may choose from a number of disciplines or paths. These involve various degrees of difficulty. The goal of each is to accumulate karma through one's obedience. The result of an obedient life is rebirth into a higher existence and, ultimately, nirvana.	The scripture common to almost all Hindus is the Bhagavad Gita, the story of Krishna's incarnation. Worship is broad and ill-defined. Many Hindus visit the Ganges River, believing it has spiritual power. Hindus hope to die at Benares. Hindus are widely known for their caste system and their belief that all forms of life are sacred.
Human beings are slaves to their cravings and their attachment to things. Actually, everything in life is impermanent, and ownership is an illusion. The inability to accept these facts causes craving, and craving causes suffering.	By accepting the impermanence of all things, people can eliminate desire and achieve "passionless peace." This is the state of nirvana, which releases one from the cycle of samsara (birth and rebirth). To reach this state, one must follow the Eightfold Path.	At age four, every Buddhist boy goes through a highly symbolic ritual and becomes a monk. He may choose to remain a monk as an adult. Women have an inferior role, and only males can achieve nirvana. There are two sects of Buddhism: Hinayana and Mahayana. Another group, Zen Buddhists, ignore the doctrines of Buddhism and emphasize meditation.

Religion	Origin and Location	Beliefs The Supreme Being
Judaism	At one time exclusively God's chosen people, the Jews have a history of persecution, homelessness, and mass execution. A religious Jew is one who accepts the teachings of Judaism. Although Judaism began, of course, in Israel, its adherents are dispersed throughout the world today.	The cornerstone of Judaism is the Shemah: "Hear, O Israel: The Lord our God is One Lord." Everything centers on God. He is a moral God Who demands reverence and obedience, but He is also a God of love. He shares His glory with no other. Adherents of traditional Judaism believe they are still exclusively God's chosen people.
Islam	There are about 700 million Muslims in the world today. Since its founding in the seventh century A.D., Islam has spread rapidly, influencing every race and continent. Its roots lie both in the animistic, polytheistic religion of the nomadic Arabs and in Judeo-Christian teachings. Both affected its founder, Muhammad.	Among the early Arabs, Allah was the supreme God. For Muslims, Allah is the one and only, the God of absolute unity, who sees all, knows all, is all-powerful and unchanging. He shares his glory with no other.

| | Beliefs | |
The Human Predicament	**The Way of Salvation**	**Scriptures Distinctive Practices**
The Jews have endured tremendous suffering for centuries. Their view of the human predicament is that of the Old Testament. All human beings are sinners in need of a savior. Suffering is the result of sin. The world is in a state of chaos, rushing headlong toward destruction.	Adherents of Judaism anticipate the coming of the Messiah, who will restore the Jewish people and, through them, the world. Until his coming, obedience to the law is the only way of salvation. This obedience will bring righteousness in this life and will give eternal life in heaven to the faithful.	Although Jews believe all of the Old Testament, the Torah (the law) is by far the most important part. The Talmud contains sixty-three books which explain the Torah. Jewish boys are highly educated while girls are taught to be homemakers. Judaism emphasizes family and community.
Human beings must accept the teachings of the last true prophet, who taught that one must submit to Allah or be lost. The greatest sin is refusal to acknowledge and praise Allah, unwillingness to submit to his perfect will. Allah is supreme and deserving of constant praise. He rewards the submissive with a heaven of sensual delights and punishes the disobedient and irreverent with a hell of gruesome agonies.	In order to gain eternal life in heaven, one must practice complete submission to the will of Allah. This includes obedience to the Five Pillars and the Shari'a, an extremely strict code of ethics, morality, and civil and criminal law.	Islam accepts four scriptures: the Torah, the Psalms, the gospel of Jesus, and the Koran. Only the Koran is considered Allah's complete revelation. Muslims are known for their prayers, said five times daily. They also go to the mosque every Friday at noon. They give alms to all who ask, fast for the month of Ramadan, and attempt to travel to Mecca at least once in their lives.